Tim Pole has worked in the field of sales and marketing for over 30 years. He spent 27 years in Australia and now lives in Northampton, England.

BE YOURSELF

*The No-Nonsense Guide to Living
Effectively*

Timothy Pole

ELEMENT

Shaftesbury, Dorset • Rockport, Massachusetts
Melbourne, Victoria

© Element Books Limited 1997
Text © Timothy Pole 1997

First published in Great Britain in 1997 by
Element Books Limited
Shaftesbury, Dorset SP7 8BP

Published in the USA in 1997 by
Element Books, Inc.
PO Box 830, Rockport, MA 01966

Published in Australia in 1997 by
Element Books Limited
and distributed by
Penguin Australia Ltd
487 Maroondah Highway,
Ringwood, Victoria 3134

Cover design by The Bridgewater Book Company
Page design by Roger Lightfoot
Typeset by Bournemouth Colour Press, Parkstone, Poole, Dorset
Printed and bound in Great Britain by
Creative Print and Design (Wales), Ebbw Vale

British Library Cataloguing in Publication data available

Library of Congress Cataloging in Publication data available

ISBN 1-86204-019-2

CONTENTS

For my brother Tony and his wife Julie for
simply being there when I needed them most

ACKNOWLEDGEMENTS

I am grateful to many people over the years who have taken time out of their busy schedules to share their thoughts with me on the subject of their own lives in particular and the nature of human potential in general. I am now able to appreciate the persistent prodding of close friends who kept urging me to put these ideas down on paper. Terrie Clements who picked them up and read them first deserves a special, personal, thank you.

PREFACE

The poor become rich, the sick become well, the lonely find friendship, a family unites, failures find success and solutions are found for pressing problems – is this fantasy, fiction or fact?

As a young man, I used to disbelieve such stories which appeared in the popular press or simply regarded them as highly exaggerated. Over the years I have had the opportunity to talk to people from all walks of life who have experienced personally similar life-changing situations. In talking to these people, it became apparent that they possessed or had acquired certain character traits to a higher degree than was apparent in the average person. To all outward appearances they were no different from anyone else; they were simply being themselves and experiencing more success, happiness and contentment in their lives as a result.

We all possess these character traits, together with our unique talents and abilities that comprise our personal tool-kit for use in dealing with our ever-changing world. The secret appears to lie in knowing your real self better and in being yourself. The developed character traits that distinguish genuinely successful people from their less successful counterparts are outlined in this book. We have the opportunity to learn from other people's experiences rather than by learning everything through our own personal experiences in life. It would be a time-consuming, expensive and needlessly frustrating exercise for civilization if each succeeding generation had constantly to reinvent the wheel.

This book was written mainly, but not exclusively, for those who feel they may have missed their personal trains, boats or planes in life, or just happen to be waiting in the transit lounge between journeys. The real opportunities for achieving meaning in life lie within us and not in a particular occupation or situation, and by recognizing that the best way to reach the top necessarily involves getting to the bottom of things first.

I believe the words of Ralph Waldo Emerson to be true when he wrote:

> What lies behind us and what lies before us are tiny matters compared to what lies within us.

INTRODUCTION

Is there really a need for another book on how to live more effectively? The volume of books on achieving personal happiness made me wonder. Over a 30-year period I have been fortunate enough to attend countless seminars and training courses related to personal growth and development. I believe that a successful person is anyone who is simply doing their best in any area of life using the talents and abilities they have.

I have a sense, that we need to take stock periodically of what we are doing to ourselves, to each other and to the world we inhabit. Perhaps in our search for added happiness and success in life, we need new perspectives and insights to develop better life strategies. Psychologists have studied juvenile delinquents, schizophrenics, drug addicts, depressed adults, unhappy couples, drop-outs and the children of divorce, and tell us what is wrong with us and society. These experts rarely look, however, at people whose lives are actually working. Would it not be better to study individuals with happy, thriving marriages, successful children at school and demanding, stress-filled jobs, who still remain healthy, happy and contented? Conventional medicine made great progress in the field of immunization against cholera, malaria and smallpox, three of the greatest killers of all time, partly by studying those who stayed healthy while others became ill.

However most books on super achievers, excellent companies and great leaders do not look very closely at the quality of their personal lives or their overall physical and emotional well-being. We receive a great deal of well-meaning advice from psychiatrists, psychologists, social workers and other experts. I sense that they are searching for new truths or new packaging for old truths to provide us with new ways to handle our ever-changing world. My personal view is that it is possible that we have a built in set of practical principles that feel just right for us. They lead to a happy, well-balanced life and it is up to us to uncover these principles and apply them. I have observed the effect that these principles have in the lives of relatives, friends and colleagues who are extraordinary people.

I have a confession to make: most books of this type try to convince you of how much you will get out of them; I am more interested, however, in what this book may get out of you. If you are open-minded enough to read it and to try some of the suggestions for change, it has served a purpose.

1

SELF-ESTEEM

A few years ago, a friend of mine had to take home some work he needed to complete in preparation for an important meeting the following day. His five-year-old son who wanted to talk stopped him from making much headway. To gain extra time to complete his task, my friend found a magazine with a map of the world on it and tore it into a rough jigsaw. He then set his son the task of putting the world back together. Surprisingly, within three minutes his son had completed the task. When asked how he had managed to do it so quickly, the boy said that there was a picture of a man on the other side of the paper. When he joined the man together properly, the world just came out right too.

How we see our world makes all the difference, and when we see ourselves as we really are, it can have a significant impact in altering the way we view the world around us.

Self-esteem is the amount of belief you have in yourself and is a measure of your own self-acceptance. It is not dependent upon your abilities, skills or physical appearance. Each one of us is unique according to our particular set of life experiences that influence the way in which we respond or react to the world around us. Our behaviour and responses are a direct result of what has happened to us in the past. Some of us dive into new experiences enthusiastically, while others exercise more caution, weighing up the pluses and minuses first. Some people like to consult with friends and family first, and some simply shy away or retreat from new experiences altogether. Most of us lean towards a personality style whereby we place more reliance on one sense mode than on another. Some people may be more interested in what they can see or visualize, while others are excited by what they can touch and feel. Many think by talking to themselves, while others rely on their intuition or gut reactions to a situation. It follows that we possess different learning styles: visualizers prefer to observe, feelers seek hands-on experimentation, talkers like concrete facts, while the intuitive tend towards abstract concepts. There is no better or worse style, but it is useful to be aware that most of us assume that everyone thinks the same way that we do, when that is not necessarily true.

Our individual personality styles may be more imaginative, logical, practical or enthusiastic by nature. There are advantages and disadvantages to each style according to the relative strength or weakness of our reliance on each in negotiating our way through life. For example, imaginative people, who generally see things in perspective, have numerous options and recognize their potential gains. However, they may fail to see the wood for the trees, having many ideas but lacking action plans and failing to act promptly. Logical people tend to be well-organized fact gatherers who calculate probabilities well and benefit from past experiences. They may need too much evidence, be overcautious and fail to let go of the past easily. Practical people see problems as normal by gathering facts and opinions before they test their solutions according to plan. They may act without due caution and be impatient loners who do not work well with other people. Enthusiastic people tend to be active risk takers who involve others in the development of ideas and options for change. They may be disorganized, doing a number of jobs at the same time, making it hard for others to follow them.

We need to recognize that individual personality styles may vary considerably from our own, but that there is no right or wrong personality to be successful in life. It is obvious, however, that someone who can use all the personality styles to some extent when dealing with life situations has a distinct advantage. Positive self-esteem is the single most important quality that characterizes the more successful individuals in our society, regardless of their particular personality style. Successful people possess the following strengths and attributes in varying degrees:

- They have strong beliefs in certain values and principles that they are willing to defend or amend where necessary.
- They do not waste time worrying about past mistakes or being unduly anxious about what tomorrow may bring.
- They have confidence in their ability to find solutions to problems, and regard setbacks and failures as opportunities to learn and grow.
- They feel a sense of equality with others, regardless of differences in ability, social standing or culture.
- They tend to look for the good in other people and are sensitive to their needs.
- They believe they have numerous choices and act on their own initiative to bring about desired changes.

- They are capable of accepting praise without false modesty and are able to accept criticism in a positive way.

How would you feel if someone you knew and trusted telephoned you today and said, 'I hope you don't mind me calling, but I just wanted to say how much I enjoy working with you. You are terrific at your job and really support and encourage others too. Personally, I feel a lot happier and more productive whenever you are around.'? If that person was known to be sincere and genuine, how would that make you feel?

Whatever your position in a group, that call would tend to make you better at your job and a much happier person. Would you as a mother, father, teacher, student or business person actually know any more or be more skilled at your job following such a call? The obvious answer is that you would not, but that you would feel better and happier as a result of that call. The simple reason is that you have had a change of image and you now see yourself in a more positive light. An interesting change then happens as your self-image receives a boost: your confidence improves and so does your performance.

A practical real-life example clearly demonstrates the possibilities that open up following a change of self-image. Victor Serebriakoff, aged 15, was advised by his teacher to leave school and learn a trade. Victor took the advice and, for the next 17 years, as a bored manual worker, held a variety of jobs suited to his inadequate and patchy education. In 1945, at the age of 32, Victor joined the army where a routine intelligence test revealed that he had an IQ of 161. Classified as a potential officer, promoted, trained and educated, this gave him a whole new set of hopes and aspirations. A transformation took place. Owing to the change in his self-image, Victor started to behave as the genius that he was and he went on to become a high-tech industrialist, inventor, lecturer and writer. A significant highlight in the life of Victor Serebriakoff was his election as chairperson of the International Mensa Society whose members have IQ scores greater than 140. Victor did not instantly acquire a vast amount of extra knowledge, but he did acquire a new image of himself. This new image gave him the confidence to expect and get different results in his life. It makes one wonder how many people like Victor Serebriakoff there are who act as if they are ignorant simply because someone once told them that they were not very clever.

It is surprising how fragile and tender our self-esteem can be. The fear of rejection may be traced back to criticism from parents, members of our family, people at work and even our friends. The fear of being rejected arises from associating ourselves with our past mistakes. As parents, we can make the classic mistake when bringing up our children of calling them naughty boy, naughty girl, cry baby, spoiled brat or untidy little devil. While we really intend for these labels to apply to an aspect of our children's behaviour, a child takes them for a description of who they are as a person. Unfortunately, most children are unable to separate what he or she does from who he or she is. Called confusing the doer with the deed, it can have a long-term, negative effect on their personal self-esteem.

When children begin school, parents and school mates give them labels such as fatty, four eyes, smelly, ugly, stupid, or even worse names. In college, university or later in the workplace, these negative put-downs may continue with names such as egg-head, dense, boring, lazy, weirdo or drop-out.

Individuals who become subjected to an environment which is full of name-calling, labelling and put-downs can develop less than adequate self-esteem and in turn they may become critical adults themselves. This acquired fear of rejection becomes the fear of change, which causes them to seek positions where they feel safe and unchallenged. They prefer a quiet journey down the river of life in a comfortable berth aboard a boat that is stabilized against the waves of change. For them, the game of life is as good as over and their comfortable berth becomes just another boring rut. They fail to understand that a rut is simply a coffin with the ends knocked out. The words on their tombstones could read, for example: 'Born in 1945, died in 1970 and finally buried in 2015'. Given the choice about how to get to the top of an oak tree, they prefer to sit on an acorn waiting for it to grow up from under them instead of climbing the tree standing in front of them.

The fear of change translates itself into a fear of success, which is as strong as the fear of rejection caused by inadequate self-esteem. The fear of success syndrome which seems to paralyse many people, is really the fear of trying which manifests itself as resistance to change, procrastination and rationalization.

One hears conversations almost every day in which people discuss someone they know who has gained a qualification, a promotion or set up a business. Their reply invariably is: 'I could not imagine being able to find the time to do further study with my commitments', or 'I could not see myself handling the responsibilities of that job', or 'I can see how they may have made it, but it's just too risky these days.' The fact that these achievers all come from similar backgrounds and that they have somehow managed to be successful escapes the bystanders. Although they may even have read the biographies of people who have overcome major stumbling blocks and handicaps to achieve success. The doubters are simply unable to accept that the lessons could be usefully applied to their own lives. They develop the habit of looking to the past and focusing on doubts and previous mistakes, which only serves to reinforce their past failures. When looking towards the future, they imagine similar poor performances and forecast their own failure in the process. Sadly, they resign themselves to mediocrity and failure, wishing and envying their lives away. The lives of these individuals are being controlled effectively by the acceptance or rejection standards of other people.

People with low self-esteem often deliberately set unrealistically high goals and ambitions for their lives. By not really believing in the validity of their dreams and by not preparing well enough for their accomplishment, they fall short of the mark again and again. Failure then becomes set as the measure of their self-esteem and whenever they start to make any real progress or to come close to realizing their goal, it tumbles down like a house of cards. The collapse of a person's self-esteem is caused by their fear of being successful which makes them put off the necessary preparation and avoid taking the creative action which is necessary to ensure a successful result. These failures become rationalized to satisfy the internal questioning that 'How could I really have expected to be successful this time? Look how often I managed to fail in the past.'

We need to understand that our minds weigh the positive gains and desires against the negative losses or fears of any undertaking. The mind compares the pleasant feelings of success with the unpleasant feelings of failure which are based on past experiences. Our choices will depend on the relative strengths of 'Can do, want to' or 'Can't do, won't do'. The former is known as reward motivation, the latter as fear motivation; if they are evenly balanced, we tend to do nothing at all.

During a seminar, a lecturer had a builder's plank placed between two chairs about 2ft off the ground. He invited two men and a woman to walk across the plank and gave them some money for each time they could do it. This they managed three times with ease. One of the men even walked the plank backwards. The lecturer then proposed taking the plank to the top of the ten-storey building they were in and placing it across the lane-way to an adjacent building. Despite offers of fifty times as much money each, none of the three was prepared to walk the plank in its new position because the fear of failure was stronger than the reward for success. The lecturer suggested to the woman that if he was threatening to throw one of her children off the roof of the adjacent building, she would not hesitate to cross the plank. (Her reply to this suggestion was that it rather depended on which of her children he was proposing to throw off the building!)

Drugs, alcoholism and promiscuity are often symptoms of a poor self-esteem. Many passing fads are the result of individuals wanting to be themselves in defiance of parents or the establishment. Inside each rebel is a little child saying, 'You did not pay sufficient attention to me before – now I will really grab your attention.' What these people really want is attention, recognition, acceptance and love; their behaviour is really a cry for help. They are unable to accept themselves as they are and begin to act like somebody else instead. This is a pity as most people are unable to mimic someone else if they are unable to accept themselves as they really are. When we accept ourselves as we are, it is not essential that everyone instantly accepts us. It is acceptable if someone occasionally rejects us for we know that we must be true to ourselves. Individuals who have a less than adequate self-esteem may possess the following characteristics to some degree. They

- Stay dependent on others for their financial security.
- Blame others for the problems they experience.
- Wait for others to change first before they will.
- Wait to see how life turns out before making commitments.
- Become passionately interested in unimportant issues.
- Over-indulge in food, alcohol and drugs.
- Refuse help or get the wrong help.
- Begin valuing the feelings of disappointment.
- Perceive criticism as a personal insult.
- Do not feel comfortable being alone, inactive or quiet.

A primary quality possessed by quiet achievers that appears to escape other people is that we must feel love inside ourselves before we can share it with anyone else. If we lack an honest, deep, inner sense of our own value and worth as individuals, we really have little to offer or share with anyone else. However we can be dependent on others, by looking to them for our physical and emotional security, flattering them or even attempting to buy love from them. It is simply impossible to give or share an emotion with someone else unless we first possess that emotion ourselves.

The most successful people in life retain a strong belief in their own worth and value, even when they have few material possessions to sustain them. They hold fast to their dreams and believe in the validity of their ideas, their belief being stronger than the rejection or acceptance of them by other people.

Material achievements are standards of excellence in projects or products that fill a recognized human need. There is just as much value in a person before their ideas or products are accepted or manufactured as there is afterwards when they have achieved fame and fortune.

When Walt Disney had a new idea he would ask ten people at random what they thought about it. If they all gave negative responses, he would start working on his idea immediately. Walt Disney had many rejections to deal with during his lifetime as a result of seeing things differently from other people and putting everything he had into his dreams. When Walt Disney was trying to find people in Hollywood to give him financial backing for an early cartoon, *Steamboat Willie*, he was bankrupt. It is hard to imagine just how difficult it must have been in the days of silent films to sell anyone the idea of a talking mouse with a squeaky voice. However, children and adults around the world today continue to appreciate the wonderful films and magical theme-parks created by this remarkable dreamer.

So was Walt Disney a better human being when he was bankrupt and still doing the original voice of Mickey Mouse, or after he had made all those marvellous films and created those magical theme-parks? Walt Disney had the kind of self-esteem that enabled him to persevere long after others would have stopped trying. He had a self-sustaining confidence in his own abilities and dreams, and clearly understood that real value resides in the doer and not in the deed.

Self-esteem is the honest value we place on ourselves

as individuals, based on a realistic assessment of our own aptitudes, talents and abilities. Thus we see clearly where we are now and where we hope to be in the future. We can then take the right steps to harmonize these elements by making any necessary adjustments in our thinking processes.

Our self-esteem defines the limits of our potential achievements in life. We cannot perform for an extended period of time in a manner which is inconsistent with the way we actually see ourselves. Each one of us is where we are today because of the information planted in our minds in the past. We change where we will be in the tomorrows of our lives by the information which we allow to be planted in our minds today.

In a laboratory experiment, rats were placed in a maze of tunnels, one of which contained food. They soon discovered which tunnel that was. When the food was moved to another tunnel, initially they went down the one which originally contained the food, but they rapidly explored the others until they found their reward again. So with human beings, the rapid pace of life today requires the ability to adapt to changing circumstances quickly. Unfortunately, some people are more set in their ways than the rats in this experiment, and they continue to head down the same old tunnel, long after their reward has moved elsewhere. They may become frustrated and disillusioned, or give up altogether in the search for their particular rewards in life.

We see our doctors regularly for a complete physical check-up to ensure our physical well-being. We should also give ourselves a regular 'check-up from the neck up' to confirm that we are heading down the right tunnel which contains our particular rewards. A low self-esteem, which is usually referred to as an inferiority complex, arises partly from comparing our worst features to someone else's best features. Some individuals may have particular qualifications for a job or profession, but you, too, have special aptitudes, abilities and life experiences. Of course, you can admire the abilities of others, but if you chose to devote the same amount of time and effort to being yourself and developing your own talents, you could achieve far more in your life. Even if we could instantly acquire the talents of the people we profess to admire, we would not benefit greatly by it unless we use fully the abilities we already possess.

A coin and an ingot of gold have exactly the same value if they lie undisturbed at the bottom of the ocean. Only when the coin and ingot are raised to the surface and put to good use, do the differences become apparent. To be competent members of our generation, we should realize that human beings become frustrated and discontented to the extent that they avoid doing the things they know they really should be doing.

A healthy self-esteem is simply the basis of our ability to love others unconditionally and to pursue worthwhile goals without fear. An alternative way to view fear, based on its initial letters, is False Education Appearing Real. The things we fear most in life are those which appear new or are unfamiliar to us at first glance. It is perfectly natural to experience some degree of anxiety when faced with significant changes in our lives. Meeting new people, starting a new job, moving to a new area or having to learn new skills, are all potentially stressful situations. The darker fears which may prevent some individuals from moving forwards at all from the familiar known to the unfamiliar unknown, need light shedding on them. We should explore any fears we have in detail and learn as much as possible about our greatest fears. In the light of certain knowledge, the darkness of fear becomes a visible light which shows us the way to move forwards. A healthy self-esteem is not self-conceit, nor is it related to self-gratification, which is a purely materialistic type of self-worship. The strangest human disease must be conceit because it makes everyone ill except the person who actually has it. Self-esteem comes from the internal acceptance of ourselves as we are now, seeing ourselves as worthwhile, growing, yet imperfect individuals with a right to be here. We need to be fully aware of the fact that although we are not all born with equal physical and mental abilities, we are born with equal rights to expect and deserve the best from ourselves, based on the internal standards we set for our lives.

Someone who is using all of the talents and skills they have and is earning a reasonable living is a success. Another person who is earning twice that a year but who is capable of earning twice that amount again is a relative failure. Money is not the true measure of a person's real value, but is a relative yardstick that society uses to value each individual's contribution. There are many selfless individuals whose love of others makes monetary rewards a secondary consideration to what they do. In my experience, most people who say that they are not interested in earning more money will generally lie about other things in their lives, too. Some people talk of cold, hard cash, although it is really warm and soft to the touch. My wife Usha says that it is also perfectly colour co-ordinated to go with any outfit she happens to be wearing while she is shopping. If we utilize all we have to make the most of our lives, we can count ourselves among the quiet achievers of our generation.

2

CREATIVITY

Human beings are the only living organisms on earth created without built-in systems that automatically enable them to live happy, contented and prosperous lives. Birds, animals, fish, reptiles and even insects instinctively know what they must do and how they must respond to ensure that they flourish and survive. We too have our share of basic survival instincts too, but we also possess far more marvellous and elaborate abilities than any other creature on this planet.

Although we are not born with detailed instructions on how to achieve the things we desire, we do have wonderful creative imaginations to help us. It is fundamentally important to our growth that we hold clear images in our minds of positive, well-adjusted, successful individuals. We can then seek to develop those attributes which will help us to make the most of our lives. We should seek to associate on a daily basis with people who are cheerful optimists and avoid spending too much time in the company of negative people. It also helps to associate with those who are cleverer and more intelligent than we are and who possess the character traits we would like to develop in ourselves. We gain much of our thinking, manners and habits from the people around us, whether they are good or bad for us.

Creative thinking thrives when we move in a circle of people who provide mutual stimulation, positive feedback and constructive criticism. We should seek to educate ourselves with materials that emphasize the positive values of society and not the less desirable aspects of humanity. You should avoid the temptation to read or view materials that show the worst aspects of human nature. Whenever we see our fellow human beings degraded, we often feel ourselves to be devalued at the same time.

We have long ceased to be members of nomadic tribes in search of food or following herds in the continual quest for new pastures. Since we are no longer hostages to our changing environment, we need different plans and instructions to help us to adapt to our more settled existence. The quiet achievers choose helpful role models and take on clear values as guides and outlines for their progress. They know that the simplest and quickest route to success lies in emulating the characteristics that work for other successful people. Their less successful counterparts have unsuitable role models and uncertain values which act as hurdles and barriers to the achievement of worthwhile goals.

Each of us is born without any real sense of who we are as individuals. We can compare ourselves to a blank video camera cassette on which the essential key messages and images are missing. Through the process of observation and real-life experiences, we build up our personal collection of sounds, pictures and sensory impressions. These impressions are continuously recorded by our personal video cameras. In the early part of our lives we are similar to the first-time buyer of a video camera. We film anything and everything about us without giving it very much thought. As time passes, we become more selective about which images, sounds and sensations we prefer to record. The scope of our preferences varies according to the location and variety of sets available, and the quality of the actors and actresses who have various roles in our lives. This recorded information and preference list becomes who we think we are in relation to other people who inhabit the world around us.

Our view of the world is filtered and coloured through the image we hold of ourselves in the mind's eye. The process of comparing the information from our senses to the image we hold decides how we respond or react to different situations. When our self-image is cared for and well cultivated, it provides fertile ground for the seeds of happiness and success to grow and flourish. When this same self-image is undernourished or neglected, it provides difficult soil that produces troublesome behaviour patterns, low achievement and general unhappiness. There is a saying to the effect that 'You become what you eat'; I believe that we could also add, 'You become what you watch and think.'

Too many people exist on a mental diet of second-rate newspapers, magazines, books and television. Much of it is pure escapism, some of which it is designed to shock our systems or, even worse, to appeal to the lower instincts in human nature. The bulk of the material we have available to read and view is a type of mental junk food that leads inevitably to mental malnutrition. This mental garbage can have adverse effects on our emotional state and give us a negative mental outlook on life. At one end of the scale we are exposed to the anti-social behaviour of the uncouth, the bizarre and the mentally incompetent. At the other end of the scale, we have the super models who are always more beautiful, and heroes who are always stronger and more handsome than we are. It is hardly surprising that if ordinary human beings choose to compare themselves with these artificial media creations, they come to regard themselves as less than perfect. We are not super models and we are never likely to be, yet some people never stop trying to copy these false images. Some people are actively engaged in trying to be super models when they should be themselves while following the examples of role models who are realistic and achievable.

The media struggle to gain our attention generally and to influence our buying power in particular is intense. We have grown up in an era in which the television set has become a window to the world beyond the homes of many people. Television has a powerful effect in shaping our opinions and can even provide the basis for many of our values and beliefs. By the time that many children leave school, they will have spent 50 per cent more time watching television than in the classroom or having real-life experiences with families or friends. It would be unfair to place all the blame on the television industry for this sad state of affairs. We still retain the ability to exercise our own choices about the amount of time we spend and what we choose to watch as our steady daily diet of television programmes. The quality of television programming is often a reflection of the way the programme-makers evaluate the average family's interests and preferences. A popular television series is based on the contestants' ability to recall detailed information about programmes that were shown many years ago. Most of us can complete the last line of commercials when prompted by the first few words or remember popular advertising jingles if someone whistles a few notes, even if they have not appeared for years.

Have we ever considered the possibility that if a 60-second commercial by repeated viewing can and does influence our purchase of products and services, is it possible that a 30-minute soap opera by repeated viewing can influence the choices we make in our lives and actually sell us a lifestyle? Do we find ourselves identifying with the problems of particular characters and relate them to our personal life situations or those of close friends? Does watching the incompetent, inept, immoral and often criminal behaviour of these characters make us feel smug or self-satisfied with our own efforts in life? When these programmes get you hooked to tuning in the following day so that you will not miss the latest action, you could have developed a real problem of your own. Although viewers say that the programmes are harmless, that they do not believe any of the stories and that watching them is something to do, imagine how productive it would be if they spent that time using their creative imaginations to plan a better future for themselves instead of solving the fictional problems of others. Many apparently intelligent adults suffer withdrawal symptoms if they take a holiday and miss their favourite soap operas. A major concern on their return home is to find out what has happened to the characters while they were away.

Many recent studies have revealed how our imaginations and learning patterns are altered by the programmes we choose to watch repeatedly. The scientists who have conducted extensive research in this area reveal that the process by which this happens is relatively simple. In the first place, we are exposed to new characters and their behaviour patterns as they deal with everyday problems. We then acquire some of these new behavioural patterns to deal with situations in our own daily lives. The last but most crucial step in this process is that we adopt these new behaviours as if they were actually our own.

One of the most important aspects of human development that we need to understand and appreciate is the powerful effect that repeated viewing and verbalization has in shaping our futures. While the information goes in almost unnoticed on a daily basis in what seems to be a completely harmless manner, we do not respond to it until much later. We are then unable to recognize that the true origins or reasons for our responses or reactions to situations resemble those we have seen on television. Our value systems are therefore being effectively shaped and formed without any real awareness on our part of what is actually happening in this vitally important area of our daily lives.

As a result of knowing these facts we can become more aware of the need to exercise caution about the information we choose to allow others to plant in our minds. Wherever possible, we should choose to view, listen and read material that forms a creative and helpful part of our routine mental daily diet. If you suspect that you may be suffering from mental malnutrition because of the rubbish dumped into your head in the past, a cure is available which does not involve painful removal of that material. The best way to deal with mental malnutrition is to make a quality decision to bury all this rubbish deeper and deeper beneath layers of clean, fertile material in the future.

What if it were possible for us to change television channels to one inside our own heads where our minds were video cameras instead of television sets? What if it were possible for us to produce our own programmes, to write our own scripts, to rehearse our roles and then video them for our own enjoyment both now and in the future? Well, we can and we do all these things every moment of our waking and sleeping lives. It seems that our minds have a real problem distinguishing between an actual life experience and one which is repeatedly and vividly imagined. A real understanding of the power of the imagined experience is the key that unlocks the door to understand human behaviour patterns. The power of the imagined experience also provides us with a valuable tool for changing our own behaviour patterns for the better.

The majority of our everyday decisions are based on the information that we have stored away about ourselves during the past. This information that we see as the truth about ourselves and our abilities may be inaccurate or simply out of date. The sources of our beliefs and knowledge are a combination of hearsay from family and friends, real-life experiences and information which we have collected from books, newspapers, radio and television. Every day of our lives we have the opportunity to program our imaginations to work for us or against us. We may also grant permission to other people which allows them to program our imaginations to work for or against our own interests.

During brain surgery it is possible to operate with the patient fully conscious during some procedures and this is necessary in certain circumstances. Much of our understanding about which areas of the brain are responsible for memory and the learning processes has been discovered during this type of surgery. Neurosurgeons insert a fine metal probe with a tiny electric current running through it into various parts of the brain and ask the patient what they are experiencing as a result of the electrical stimulation. Some individuals are able to recall in vivid detail previously forgotten events from their childhood, such as birthday parties. Not only do they see all the people who were present and recall every detail of the conversations which took place, but they can recall in minute detail their actual surroundings. The most remarkable fact is that they can actually smell the flowers around them and taste the foods they ate as if it were happening in the present. These individuals are doing more than remembering past events – they are actually reliving them, which makes us realize the importance of what we choose to allow into our own heads.

We can choose to review many of our successful past performances in the realms of our imagination, which helps us to perform better today. We can also focus on the negative aspects of our past performances, which hampers our ability to give a good performance today. We can also preview in our creative imaginations forth-coming attractions in which we see and hear ourselves giving award-winning performances. We have the abili-ty to practise and perform situations repeatedly in our imaginations without the external pressures of the real event. This ability to plan and fantasize our futures by experiencing every colour, word, touch and smile in vivid detail has real value for us. The power of the cre-ative imagination is something we can all learn to use more effectively by taking the time to relax and focus on positive images from past experiences, and by simulat-ing a successful project or lifestyle as if it were actually happening today.

The people who would derive most benefit from this activity say that they are far too busy to indulge in such idle day-dreaming. They are highly resistant to inquiries about the amount of time they spent sitting in front of the television, aimlessly scanning newspapers or half-listening to sports broadcasts. If someone gave them a million pound racehorse, they would ensure that it had the best nutrition, the right exercise and received the first-class training it so richly deserved. Anyone who would do that for a million pound racehorse and not do that much for themselves has a real problem with their personal self-image.

Whether we care to accept it or not, we are the writers, producers and stars of our own true-life videos. We determine whether ours will be a starring role in an award-winning epic or a bit part in a television soap opera. These true-life videos are the stories of our individual lives which we create in the realms of our own imaginations. We have far more control over the course of our lives than we may have previously thought possible. We are responsible adults and understand that this is true of everyone's life, because who we see in our imaginations will always govern our world. The finished video, whether it makes us sad and anxious or happy and content, lies in our ability to create the world we want to inhabit in our imaginations.

Although some people claim that they have difficulty in creating pictures in their mind's eye, yet only those born blind are unable to exercise this ability. Lack of practice can weaken this natural gift, so we may need to reactivate it through simple exercises. If you ask a small child to make up a story about any picture, you will quickly realize how fertile our imaginations used to be. We are all born with vivid imaginations but are taught at school how to reason logically. As children we were told repeatedly to stop day-dreaming and to concentrate on our lessons. As a result, our creative imaginations were gradually reduced. The over-emphasis on using the rational, reasoning left side of the brain can adversely affect our ability to use the intuitive, artistic right side. To be fully functional human beings we need to integrate both sides of the brain and become whole brain thinkers.

The left side of the brain is like a digital computer which can only deal with a single input, while the right side is like the analogue computer which can deal with many inputs at once. The left side of the brain is logical, reasoning, analytical, calculating and associated with our memories. The right side is creative, imaginative, rhythmic, intuitive and associated with our emotions. To realize our full potential we need to rediscover and restore power to the right side of our brains. Why is the power to influence the course of our lives through creative visualization largely ignored or not understood by so many people?

The answer appears to lie with our almost obsessive reliance on the power of logical thinking to the point where we spend virtually no time at all using our creative imaginations. Creative visualization is not a substitute for skills or training, but it can enhance our ability to perform far better than we previously thought possible. Many famous artists and scientists credit their greatest inspirational moments to periods when they were not actively thinking about their work at all. With all the emphasis on left brain activity, it is quite clear that creative thinking is primarily a function of the right side of the brain.

Creativity is not only useful to artists, poets and writers, it is also an invaluable asset in the world of business. The solution-orientated, creative-thinking business person has a real advantage in the competitive arena of new ideas and their development. Children spend much of their time passively watching television instead of being actively encouraged to read and open up their imaginations by creating pictures for themselves. Many children have access to computers, but instead of using them creatively they are content to play games that improve eye and hand co-ordination but do little to stimulate their imaginations. You cannot visualize yourself passing your driving test and expect to succeed if you have failed to learn the highway code or practised reversing around corners and doing three-point turns. However, you can visualize yourself doing these things confidently and see yourself gaining your licence, which will calm any nervous feelings you may have and will greatly increase your chances of success.

One quiet achiever I know used creative visualization to overcome his natural shyness when dealing with the opposite sex. He visited a shop where a lively sales assistant to whom he was attracted always managed to show an extra interest in him beyond ordinary politeness. He was a quiet, studious person who had protective parents and mainly associated with their friends or older acquaintances. As a teenager he felt different from his contemporaries who appeared to have a capacity for spontaneous fun that he somehow lacked. Simply to engage this young lady in conversation with a view to asking her out filled him with fear, even though he saw himself as a lonely person as a result of his irrational feelings. He resolved to do something about this particular situation and put an end to his emotional isolation from others. He began to picture himself as confident and self-assured, and he rehearsed repeatedly in his imagination a simple two-way conversation with the young lady that had a successful outcome. He put his plan into action and managed to establish a rapport with her over several weeks, before eventually he was able to ask her out to dinner, which she accepted, and they became very good friends. As in the case of the video analogy, he visualized a positive outcome, wrote a script, rehearsed the action and called lights, camera and action when he was ready to do so.

We should also realize that we are our own harshest critics with the power to devastate our self-esteem through cutting remarks and pessimistic judgements of our daily performances. We should choose, therefore, to raise our self-esteem through the use of positive self-talk and more optimistic assessments of our daily performances.

Every moment of every day we are having private conversations with ourselves in our own heads. Our self-image is closely monitoring every word we say about our self and accepts what it hears and acts as if it were true. So it is obvious that when we are talking to ourselves, we should be aware of who is listening and watch the language we use.

3

3

RESPONSIBILITY

About a hundred years ago reasonable leisure time and learning privileges were available to very few people. For the large majority of people, their school days were short, and their working days and hours long. Those who worked most or all of their lives had little or no time free to improve on the cursory childhood education they received to prepare them for the occupations of adult life.

It helps us occasionally to consider how lucky we are in comparison with some people alive today who can still remember the way things used to be. Men rose from their beds before dawn, consumed an inadequate breakfast, trudged off to work and arrived home long after dark. Often they were so exhausted that they could hardly eat before they fell asleep again, the whole process being repeated six days a week. This working life started when a lad was still a teenager and for such back-breaking, mind-numbing labour he would be paid barely enough to keep the most basic of foods on the family table. The women had a hard life too, with primitive cooking facilities, no electricity, inadequate health care, and medicines that were expensive and difficult to obtain. She bore many children, was exposed to deadly diseases and, after years of unrelenting struggle, worked herself into an early grave.

With the advent of industrial democracy at the beginning of the 20th century, changes occurred which had an effect on everyone's lives. The increased productive capacity of machinery began to free many people from a life of unremitting toil. Increased years of schooling for children, reductions in the number of working hours and the years of working life, were accompanied by improvements in economic and political freedom. More and more people obtained the conditions of economic and political freedom, and it became possible for them to begin to lead the lives of free human beings.

It has taken more than 190 years of economic, political and social change to accomplish our closeness to the ideals of real freedom. Yet despite the opportunities and responsibilities this freedom offers us, some people still choose to continue to live like slaves. From the moment of our birth the fight begins against ignorance and if we do not assume our responsibilities in refusing to allow this oppressor to exercise control over us, we are enslaved.

The freedom we have through increased leisure hours provides us with ample opportunities to spend a proportion of that time responsibly in the pursuit of knowledge, wisdom and understanding. Just an hour a day spent in this way can open up a whole new outlook on life and provide us with more control over our daily lives and our environment.

If the past teaches us anything, it is that every cause produces its effects and our actions produce results. It is true for all of us that we reap what we plant, whether by thought, word or deed. It seems from the mass media that the corrupt and unscrupulous appear to flourish at the expense of the more ethical and honest members of our society. The sun may indeed shine equally on the good and bad alike, but we may rest assured that the apparent achievements of the bad are largely an illusion.

Whether we appreciate it or not, life keeps books on all of us, recording our thoughts, words and deeds which become our individual characters. We are unable to fake our real characters by changing them to suit the needs of each passing moment; they are an integral part of us that takes time to grow and develop. Each day we are actively creating our own futures for inevitably we become what we think, say and do most often. The quiet achievers know that their real rewards in life will depend entirely upon the worth and measure of the improvements they are able to make daily in themselves and in other people's lives. We say that we want additional freedom, but do we really want to pay the price that goes with it these days? The answer lies with cause and effect, and our ability or inability to accept personal responsibility for what we do today in bringing about tomorrow's consequences.

One of the major obstacles that stands in the way of our personal freedom is surely the overwhelming demand by many people to have their desires met instantly. These unrealistic expectations are fuelled by images of the self-styled 'beautiful people' who appear to follow their questionable life-styles with effortless ease. These demands increase because we find ourselves surrounded by advertising which methodically appeals to a fantasy world that more responsible minds resist.

A distinguishing feature of our culture appears to be that we are advertising our commitment to immaturity, falsehood and extreme gullibility. It is worth considering that advertising has been described as the art of suspending human intelligence for just so long as it takes to extract money from it. If we do not have money readily available, there are plenty of businesses which are happy to indulge our desire to have it now and pay later. The payments and interest persist, long after the impulsive desire has been satisfied and the novelty value has worn off.

To be responsible adults we should endeavour to assume debts only for those items which we deem to be essential, such as a home or a car. Then we should make a big effort to get out and stay out of debt, as quickly as possible. The philosopher Epictetus said that 'only the educated are free', to which we could add that 'only those without debt are truly free'.

The quiet achievers regard themselves and their families as individual financial corporations subject to close examination and constant review. They set personal budgets based on total projected incomes and expenditures for all the shareholder members of their family. They have regular progress meetings and ensure that everyone is involved in the decision-making process. It is important to keep a track of and to record even the smallest items of expenditure and to question the real value of all purchases to the group's position. The net worth of the group is monitored by comparing current assets to outstanding liabilities with a view to maximizing net worth.

Every year, regardless of our income, we aim to show a profit of at least 10 per cent by way of savings to allow for unknown future circumstances. Adequate provision should be made as a matter of common sense for ensuring that living standards do not drop dramatically at or before retirement age. We know that the best investment for many people is to invest any surplus funds in paying off their mortgages ahead of time. We recognize that many people do not flaunt their affluence by acquiring material objects to be admired by other equally irresponsible and immature individuals. They choose to live more simply than their counterparts on a daily basis, preferring to invest their money in income-producing products or projects to ensure their continued prosperity in the years ahead. Many individuals have champagne tastes and only beer money, which leads them to take holidays or to buy expensive cars on credit, while they may still live in rented accommodation. Responsible adults know that they must balance their financial affairs carefully to suit their particular circumstances in order to maintain a sense of personal control over their own lives.

I met someone who was a fitter and turner by trade who confided in me that he had built up and maintained what he referred to as his 'two digits' bank account. It turned out that he always had a passbook account containing the equivalent of several months' salary which he never touched, just in case he felt like resigning his job. Although he did not resign, he gained considerable psychological satisfaction from knowing that he had the financial resources to keep him going for a while if he ever gave into the temptation. We may question his attitude for setting up such an account, but he showed admirable forward planning for a possible emergency. Very few of us would invest our money in a company, either large or small, that consistently failed to show a profit or had insufficient reserve funds to meet emergencies. So how much profit did your company make last year and what is the balance of your personal 'two digits' or emergency account?

We demand instant fulfilment of our sensual desires;

we expect sex without attachments, to be loved without committing ourselves and to receive benefits from others without contributing anything in return. Any form of effort, pain, sacrifice or postponement is simply unacceptable to many people. The attitudes expressed are, 'I will try it, as long as I feel good immediately' and 'I will not enter the competition, unless I can be sure of first place' or 'I want the life-style enjoyed by the rich and famous people I see on television, and I deserve it because my parents told me I was a really special person and I want it now.'

People with such attitudes have been brought up unable to understand the meaning of the word 'no', which is interpreted by them as a 'definite maybe' for very good reasons. They remember their childhood days when, if they complained long enough and loud enough, someone always gave in and eventually gave them what they wanted. Instead of making a real effort and telling themselves that they are contenders in a race that they might actually win, they prefer to satisfy their frustrations in other ways. They seek relief from their unaccustomed denial by associating with other spoilt individuals like themselves because misery loves company. They seek instant relief for their problems by drinking too much and swallowing legal or illegal mind-altering drugs to numb the reality of the horrid world around them.

Many factors lie behind the achievements of both Germany and Japan in successfully rebuilding their countries out of the ashes following the Second World War. A key factor was the ability of their peoples to look to the future for a full return on their investments, while putting in a maximum effort in the present. The average German and Japanese worker saves up to 20 per cent of their take-home pay, which is three times more than the British. The Japanese call their take-home pay discretionary income, which to them means a choice between spending it all or saving some of it. We British refer to our take-home pay as disposable income – when we receive it, we can hardly wait to dispose of it.

It seems obvious to everyone but the British that the country is rapidly disposing of its past rewards and assets. It is not building up its investments and resources to ensure an adequate harvest for future generations. Some observers say that instead of resting on past efforts and rewards, they are actually morgaging current assets against an uncertain future.

It seems odd that some people argue constantly on the one hand for more freedom for the individual and on the other hand insist on calling for more social order. They strive continually for increased material wealth in the present, but hope in the future to obtain spiritual growth and understanding. They expect and demand greater protection from the anti-social and criminal members of society, while at the same time they express their annoyance at anything that interferes with their personal social habits. They want the government to reduce the crippling burden of taxation which they say is hindering their progress. They believe that such a reduction would enable them to assume more personal responsibility for achieving their own destinies in life. They also expect that meanwhile the government should continue to ensure their basic financial security and provide plenty of safety nets. It is obvious that they cannot have everything and the sooner they realize it the better. Whatever they say they want, they must be willing to pay the price that those choices entail.

The only sure way to foster self-reliance and personal

responsibility is to recognize and identify with the number of alternative choices open to us in a free society. Ultimately, freedom of choice presents us with two fundamental decisions to make about any circumstances which face us. We should either accept things as they are or accept our share of personal responsibility for bringing about the changes that we say we want to happen.

If we find ourselves asking why 'they' are not acting to change a situation we are unhappy about, it helps to recall that in reality 'they' are no different from ourselves. Instead of waiting for other people to take action, the quiet achievers say, 'I know what I am going to do about...' whatever happens to concern them. If we are tempted to point a finger in someone else's direction, it pays to remember that there are always three times as many fingers pointing back at us.

The happiest and most competent people are those who believe that they exercise a strong measure of control over their own lives. They choose more appropriate and realistic responses to whatever life experiences they meet along the way. These individuals learn to stand or bend to the winds of inevitable change with far less apprehension and stress. They learn valuable lessons from past mistakes which they regard as opportunities for future growth and change. They do not create unnecessary obstacles to future progress by dwelling too long on past errors and mistakes. They spend more time living in the present instead of wasting valuable energy worrying unduly about what may happen in the future.

Negative people, on the other hand, believe in fate or luck and that it could be the wrong time or wrong place to attempt anything new. They need precise astrological guidance and favourable biorhythm charts before they make any significant decisions about their future. They feel that the system is working against them and that no one really understands or cares about their unique, special problems. These people are more prone to give in to doubt, worry and fears about their individual lives. This negative approach to life means that they face greater physical hardships and emotional problems as a result.

If we want to become mature, self-reliant adults, we need to have some guidelines and to be true to ourselves by being different. We can be different from the crowd if we adopt higher standards of conduct in our personal and business lives. Furthermore, we can be cleaner and better groomed than the people around us. It is far better to arrive at a function or meeting looking slightly better than slightly worse than everyone else. We can be different from the rest by putting more time and effort into all we do, regardless of how small or humble the job may be. Every job we do takes on more dignity and meaning if we simply do it to the best of our ability. And we can be different by taking the carefully calculated risk to improve our chances of success. The biggest risk in life is to wait for others to do something or to become dependent on other people for our security.

Our greatest security will come through careful planning and prompt action, and by embracing the risks that will gain us our independence. We know that no one else can really spoil our enjoyment of life – we have to give them our permission to do that. We use sunshine from within to warm us and lighten the road which lies ahead. We choose the things that matter most to us each moment of the day. We prefer to respond positively to the people we meet every day rather than to react to what they have to say. What matters most to us is the joy of living and the acceptance of personal responsibility to bring effective change into our lives.

We should not avoid tackling the hardest and most challenging things we need to do in our lives until later. Rather, we should place the more difficult tasks at the top of our agenda and begin to work on them immediately. We should be aware of the fact that our rewards and personal satisfaction will come after we have made a real effort to do the job properly.

We hear frequent references to the ordinary, average person in our society from social scientists, politicians and the media. These ordinary, average people are seen as a large group of individuals who have similar ideas, desires, wants and earning power. This insatiable urge by government and commercial organizations to sort and label individuals into convenient, manageable groups appears endless. It is almost impossible to avoid the many opinion surveys and questionnaires which are designed to measure even the most trivial habits of the average person in the street. Many individuals now perceive that being an ordinary and average individual is a sought-after status symbol indicating mutual worth and value. Some people worry if they appear to be below average; others worry about being above average because it might isolate them from their group. In reality, there is no such thing as an ordinary, average person; it only appears that way because so many people are busy acting as if they are ordinary and average when in reality they are not. Many people believe that labels such as 'ordinary' and 'average' accurately describe material objects and then wrongly try to apply them to people.

We may label tall, green, leafy objects as trees and, because some appear different, label them as oaks or by whatever name we choose to distinguish them. An expert might label and describe the functions of different parts of a tree in great detail and still be none the wiser in knowing what a tree really is. Trees do not limit their own growth potential by conforming to the labels we choose to identify them with; unlike some people, they simply become all the tree they can possibly be.

Valuable insights about individual motivation are gained during job interviews. Many individuals focus their attention on pension schemes, holiday entitlements, sickness benefits, flexitime and the length of meal breaks. They ask how quickly they can move upwards to a better job than the one they are applying for at the moment. They have seen high-speed lifts travel up the outside of big city office buildings and they expect to ride in one to the chief executive's suite on the top floor. They are disappointed to learn that the high-speed lift is always out of order in the real world of business and that they will have to climb the stairs one at a time like everyone else.

We should tell prospective employers what we are able to offer them which will enhance their business before we inquire about the rewards and benefits we hope to receive. We are well aware that our true rewards in life will depend upon the quality and amount of contribution we are prepared to make. By cultivating great ideas within that will help us and other people, we will all become happier, more prosperous individuals as we ascend the stairway to the top floor.

4

WISDOM

In ancient Rome, successful people took a particular pride in the appearance of their homes and the places in which they worked. They took special interest in the items that they chose to beautify and adorn the interior of these buildings. One measure of personal status was how many statues of various gods were displayed in your home or place of work. The increasing demand for statues meant that being a sculptor was a popular and lucrative craft. When demand exceeded supply, some sculptors became slip-shod in their work. In earlier times, they had rejected marble with cracks in it and threw out statues that were accidentally damaged. Later, however, the cracked or chipped areas were filled with a mixture of marble dust and wax to hide these flaws. This remodelling technique became so good that the statue-buying public had difficulty in noticing the flaws and imperfections until after they had made their purchase. This practice became so widespread that the Romans had severe doubts about the integrity of the whole sculpting craft. The more expert sculptors who took considerable pride in producing fine-quality, authentic statues met to find a way of restoring public confidence. The expert craftsmen chose to display a sign which read *Sina Cere* to distinguish them from their less scrupulous brethren. If someone wanted a fine-quality, authentic statue without flaws, they would visit the forum in Rome and look for the sculptors' workshops that displayed the *Sina Cere*, or without wax, sign.

Whatever we are doing, we are always looking for those items or individuals that represent the genuine article. Of all the qualities we appreciate most in other people, sincerity, or those without wax, is top of the list.

Practical wisdom is simply the combination of honesty and knowledge applied to our daily activities. A person's honesty or dishonesty provides a clear example of the law of cause and effect in motion. Dishonest people may lie, cheat or steal from others if they choose to misuse their talents. It requires almost as much time and effort to succeed in the wrong direction as it does to go in the right one. Dishonest people get a thrill from doing the wrong thing without being caught and can become hooked on the excitement. The material gains which are achieved in this way may become secondary to the adrenaline-charged feelings of excitement and power. These criminals may develop feelings of superiority regarding their ability to evade detection and outwit the law. They see their victims as fools to be taken advantage of, because they believe that if they don't steal from them, someone else will. Unknown to them, an internal time-bomb is slowly ticking away and at some time, in some place, and somehow when they least expect it, the person and their house of wax will melt to reveal the fraud inside.

The sad fact about many people locked up inside our prisons is that they have the talents and abilities that would have enabled them to have succeeded on the outside. The people who are living inside their houses of wax have not only inflicted pain and suffering on their victims and on those they say they love, but they have also defrauded themselves. These frauds operate at all levels in society, just one step in front of the law, with their creditors just one step behind them. The following true story from the Roaring Twenties shows that some people will never learn from the lessons the past has to offer until it is too late.

Arthur Barry, a jewel thief with an international reputation, was regarded by some as the greatest 'cat' burglar of all time. He was a connoisseur of fine art and was very selective when it came to choosing his victims. Only the top names in society were robbed by this gentleman thief and it became almost a status symbol to have been robbed by him, much to the embarrassment of the police. Eventually, Barry was caught while carrying out a robbery and in a shoot-out with the police he received three bullet wounds. Lying on the floor in agony, with glass splinters in his eyes, he is alleged to have said, 'I am never going to do this any more.' Incredibly, he escaped from police custody and remained at large for three years until a jealous lover turned him over to the police. Arthur Barry served an 18-year sentence and when he was released settled anonymously in a small New England town. He lived an exemplary life and eventually became leader of a local veterans' organization. Somehow it became known that this famous jewel thief was living in the town and he was besieged by reporters asking every kind of question imaginable. One journalist asked Barry if he could remember from whom he had stolen the most, to which he replied, 'The man I stole most from was Arthur Barry. I could have been a successful businessman and a contributing member of society. Instead, I chose the life of a thief and spent two-thirds of my adult life behind prison bars.'

We have all met people who are insincere, greedy, bad-tempered or simply dishonest in their dealings with others. Their undesirable characteristics are quickly noticed by those about them and their relatively small failings prevent them from ever reaching their full potential. These negative shortcomings or acquired bad attitudes could be overcome easily if people paid attention to them and accepted responsibility for getting rid of these self-imposed obstacles to progress. It is interesting to note how many of these individuals hang on to their negative attributes as if they were their most treasured personal possessions. They refuse steadfastly to consider reading self-help books, to attend training courses or even to learn by observing the genuinely successful individuals around them. If someone points out to them that successful people are generally optimists with positive mental attitudes, they say that they would be too if they had other people's jobs and incomes. They stubbornly refuse to accept that some people are successful, in my opinion, primarily because they made the effort to acquire the right characteristics and mental attitudes in the first place. Failure has become set as the way of life of people with shortcomings, and they offer numerous plausible reasons and excuses as examples of their fortitude in facing their peculiar difficulties to anyone who is willing to listen. Life is the greatest do-it-yourself project that people will ever undertake, but some individuals insist that they are not in control of events and make themselves unhappy watching other people moving towards success and happiness.

There are many paths to success and most people

follow the one their natural instincts tend to lead them along. For the fraud and the thief, the rewards of success prove to be hollow, unsatisfactory victories. The sincere and honest quiet achievers see a happier side to life along the way to achieving their goals. Each one of us has the power to choose to stay as we are at present or change ourselves for the better. The past is dead and need not dictate our tomorrows; the future is an illusion which need not unduly concern us. All that remains is this vital moment called today, where we can learn valuable lessons from the past, plan a better future for ourselves and give of our best to all we do.

Knowledge is fast bringing about an information revolution, with changes as dramatic as those which occurred during the Industrial Revolution. Science- and technology-based industries are supplanting the more labour-intensive industries of the past. Knowledge is the fuel that is needed at the frontiers of tomorrow as brain power takes over from muscle power. As muscle power assumes a reduced role in our purely physical survival in the future, our ability to communicate on an intellectual basis will become more important. The rapid technological progress we are all experiencing will inevitably produce some human technological fall-out along the way.

We need to communicate our willingness to assist those who are adversely affected to adapt to these inevitable changes. We will need to work closely together to find fair and reasonable solutions to these problems. One of the obstacles we face in trying to work with each other intellectually lies in our ability or inability to express our thoughts and feelings in words. The frustration which is felt by some at their inability to express their real thoughts and feelings clearly can and does lead to physical violence. Regardless of education, most of us use on average around 400 words in about 80 per cent of our everyday conversations. The average unabridged English language dictionary contains well over 450,000 words. With all the words we have available for use in communication, we prefer to restrict ourselves to using just 0.1 of 1 per cent of them regularly. If we were to learn just five or ten new words every day for one year, we would find ourselves among the most well-spoken people.

Aptitude testing reveals the major part that vocabulary plays in predicting our future success in many occupations, regardless of formal education. Research spanning 80 years assures us that this primary aptitude for success in life is not understood at all by 95 per cent of the world's population. A wide vocabulary which implies a broad general knowledge is characteristic of quiet achievers in all walks of life.

Opportunities for increasing our vocabulary include reading books that widen our knowledge, and listening to good speakers on the radio and to discussions about unfamiliar topics. The *Reader's Digest* offers busy people the chance to improve their general knowledge and word power at the same time. Educational television programmes provide an easy way to acquire knowledge in new areas. We might consider the benefits to be gained from joining one of the many public speaking groups throughout the country. Public speaking is one of the safer things to do in life – no one has literally died on their feet while speaking. It is estimated that only 5 per cent of the population will read self-help books or listen to educational recordings in any one year. This fact alone makes you, the reader of this particular book, a member of a reasonably select band of individuals. If we spent the same amount of time that is spent in commuting to and from work listening to educational tapes, it has been estimated that we could earn the equivalent of a university or college degree in just five years.

If we choose to continue learning throughout our lives, we will gain knowledge and insight about our natural talents and acquire the skills needed to take advantage of them. By creating the space to read, listen and watch creative material, we will be able to express our thoughts and feelings more clearly to other people. We can choose to associate personally or through books with the best role models that are available to assist our growth. Our personal world and the people in it are not the limits of our capacity to change and to grow. Through books we can choose to keep company with the greatest thinkers and the most influential writers the world has ever known.

Every person we meet is in some way superior to us, but we too have our unique talents and special abilities. We may feel ourselves to be square pegs in round holes in our present employment and find greater fulfilment in outside interests and hobbies. We should consider the value that intelligence and aptitude testing might have for us in showing where our strengths lie. Many people are pleasantly surprised to find that they are more intelligent and capable than they at first imagined. Aptitude testing can show us the direction in which our intelligence and personalities are most likely to bear fruit.

If we have a particular talent and do not use it, we have failed. If we use only some of our talent, we are partial failures. If we manage to use all of our talents, we will experience a satisfaction that is unknown to many people. Far too many people go to their graves with most of their music still left in them because they have been too busily engaged in playing someone else's tunes. They wonder to themselves later what would have happened if only they had summoned up the courage to turn the dreams of their youth into reality.

Be yourself by not letting that happen to your particular talents because it is never too late to try a new beginning or to follow a different path in life. All of us are created with a least one particular talent that we can turn from a piece of natural quartz into a finely polished gemstone with a little time and effort. If we display our new-found talents modestly to others, their genuine interest will encourage us to bring forth more of our natural abilities. We know that practical wisdom is not a contest about how many words we actually know. Words simply provide us with the means to express ourselves honestly and openly to other people. There are specialists who seem to delight in using the language which is peculiar to their field, a language whose words put us at a disadvantage. We should choose our words with care so that the listener can really understand what we are trying to say in language that shows we are sincere. Wisdom also depends upon the honest and open estimation of the real talents and abilities we have. We should understand that it is better to accept a lower position in life and be asked to move up in the world than to overestimate our abilities and be asked to step down. Being wise depends even further upon our making a determined effort to use our abilities as fully as they were intended to be.

Many people prefer to pursue money, power and pleasure as ends in themselves. Yet we are all aware through the media of 'stars' – the rich and famous – who have achieved material possessions in abundance, only to begin the search for intuition, faith and reason to add real meaning to their lives. The quiet achievers seek out those who are wiser and deeper than themselves, either personally or through books, to gain valuable insights and to add a sense of proportion to their own lives.

Superficial people fear the wise and love ordinary people because less will be expected from them. Underachievers weigh the odds and discuss endless possibilities until they are past taking a plunge into the swirling waters of opportunity and have to make do with paddling in the calm waters of mediocrity. I have been fortunate to visit the Great Barrier Reef in Australia several times over the years and one of my favourite memories is of a trip to the reef with a character known locally in Shute Harbour as 'Captain Nemo'. While snorkelling over a particular stretch of reef which formed a lagoon around Daydream Island, Captain Nemo pointed out an interesting phenomenon to me. Inside the sheltered side of the reef which was protected from the full force of the winds and tides, the coral formations appeared somewhat pale in colour and the fish swam past me at a leisurely rate of knots. On the unprotected seaward side of the reef, the spectacular coral formations had vivid colours, and shimmering fish darted swiftly to and fro in search of food. The Marine life on the shallower and more protected side of the reef represents those people who prefer a quieter, less challenging environment. Others, though, may prefer the competitive challenge posed by the deeper, more exposed environment of the outer reef. We should make a real effort, therefore, to apply our acquired wisdom to our relationships with families, friends and colleagues at work on a daily basis.

5

~⊲⊷⊱~

PURPOSE

Visiting the Antarctic region by boat is a fascinating experience which offers many wonderful and interesting sights. Some of the most awe-inspiring of these sights are the towering icebergs which float slowly by in the distance. As you watch, you are struck by something strange which appears to happen to those icebergs. While the larger ones appear to travel in one direction, the smaller ones seem to travel in the opposite direction. The answer lies in the fact that two-thirds of an iceberg is below the surface of the water. The larger icebergs have their bases in the deeper, more powerful currents, while the smaller icebergs have their bases in the less powerful surface currents.

Individuals with a clear sense of purpose about where they want to go in life and how they are going to get there, are travelling steadily to a destination just over the horizon. Their strength of purpose is powered by a deep-down desire to achieve the goals they have charted for their lives. The usual surface squalls and unfavourable tides of life do not cause them to alter course as the depth of their desire ensures that they continue in the right direction. The less ambitious have no clear idea of what they really want in life or how they hope to obtain it. Their sense of purpose is easily influenced and changed as their desires lie just below the surface of the waves. They are content to be shifted one way and another by contrary winds, and to flow with the tide along with all the other small icebergs which float on the surface. The larger icebergs, meanwhile, continually disappear from their view towards the distant horizon, leaving the smaller icebergs to drift in aimless circles.

The quiet achievers are meaningful specifics with realistic plans, not wandering generalities with vague desires. They have written action plans for several areas of their lives which they break down into years, months and weeks. They regularly check their progress to see if they are still on course for their short-, medium- and long-range objectives. They review and amend these plans when necessary to reflect their changing circumstances but never lose sight of their real aims in life. Their goals are always just over the horizon and when they get there, they are able to see even more clearly other attractive destinations to chart their course towards.

Those who say that wandering generalities by failing to plan are planning to fail by default, are only half right as such people never actually plan anything – for them life is a series of random events. Those who do not set goals for themselves have an undeniable excuse for failing as they have never set them down on paper in the first place. This no-risk approach is like saying that it is safer for an aeroplane to stay on the ground or for a ship to stay in harbour, which at first glance may appear to be true. A second, deeper look shows that this is untrue, because ships and aeroplanes actually deteriorate faster and require more maintenance while they are on the ground or in harbour. What is true of ships and aeroplanes in this respect may be applied equally to those people who simply refuse to accept the need to plan their life journey. These same people, however, never depart on a car journey to an unfamiliar place without consulting a map and taking road conditions into account so that they can navigate with some confidence to arrive safely at their desired destination. Some people I know would rather have a tooth extracted without the benefit of anaesthetic than be asked to commit their life plans or goals to paper. Planning is really an instinctive exercise in forethought and common sense which gives us all a thread to follow through the maze of life with a measure of confidence.

If we honestly do not know where, or really care about where, we end up in life, then any road will take us there and it matters very little what we do with our lives. From information that I have read, it would seem that less than 3 per cent of the people in the Western world will reach the age of 65 with any real financial security. That means that 97 per cent of the people over the age of 65 will have to depend solely on their old age pensions to survive. This may be due partly to the adverse and difficult economic circumstances they have experienced, but there are other, deeper reasons for this situation. A surprising fact is that only some 5 per cent of people in higher income groups, such as solicitors and doctors, reach the age of 65 with adequate financial security. It seems hard to imagine that people in the higher income brackets need to depend, partly at least, on old age pensions to survive.

I was truly surprised to learn that so few people achieve any degree of financial success, regardless of their income levels, during the most productive years of their lives. Many people appear to live under an illusion that they will never lose their earning power and act as if they inhabited an immortal body. They fritter away much of their money, time and minds on irresponsible tension-relieving activities. Quiet achievers, however, prefer to invest most of their money, time and minds in interesting goal-achieving activities.

To retain a sense of purpose, quiet achievers recognize that wasting their time is really just wasting their lives. They value themselves and plan how they use their time with as much care and attention to detail as they do with their financial resources. They choose to spend more of their time doing the things they want to do instead of allowing others to set their priorities for them. They take the time to sort out their lives by dividing the 24 hours of each day to ensure that quality rather than quantity is continually at the forefront of their minds. They ask themselves, 'Is this the best use of my time?' or 'Is this really what I want to do?' and 'What do I hope to achieve from this activity?'.

We can aim to achieve a harmonious balance between work and family responsibilities, together with mental, physical and personal growth activities. We can be on our guard against the 'time bandits' by learning to say 'no' nicely to time-wasting intruders and by not engaging in things just to appear busy. We should be on time for appointments with others and expect the same courtesy in return, because those who keep others waiting steal their time. Time management is a responsible attitude towards 60 silver minutes, each of which is embedded with 60 diamond seconds that we can either use or lose 24 golden hours of each day.

Less organized people tend to waste their time on activities that have little real value to them, or they generate stress by obsessively trying to cram too much into each day. Without real values or sensible goals in their lives, time becomes an enemy that passes too slowly or goes too fast for them because it appears that they never have the right time to do the job properly. While they may complain that they haven't the time to do the job well the first time, they can always find the time to do it again the second time when it returns to them. They haven't got time because time has got them as its slave instead of being masters of their time themselves.

Many people work to get through the week and hope that they have enough money left to survive the weekend. They feel that the winds of destiny will eventually waft them effortlessly towards a safe and prosperous retirement haven. This haven is usually located on a sun-drenched, tropical island of dreams and it is known as Someday Isle. When prompted as to how they are going to attain this hoped-for life-style in the future, they usually answer, 'Somehow'!

It is quite plain that many people devote more time to planning their annual holidays and Christmas parties than they do to planning their own lives. This is why it is vitally important for us to visualize our dreams and plans with as much detail and specific information as possible. We should list the personal benefits or rewards we expect as a result of achieving each of our objectives and seek to identify foreseeable obstacles along the way. We should endeavour to find out what particular skills or knowledge we will need to acquire and which individuals or organizations we will need to work with to attain our goals. We will need to develop a specific plan of action and decide on a realistic time limit to accomplish each task we have set ourselves. Once our self-image receives these vivid and detailed goal messages on a regular basis, they will become a habit which we will then accept as part of ourselves. The quiet achievers understand that the real magic of believing starts to pay dividends once the self-image gets hooked to the success habit.

To become a London taxi driver is the dream of some people who see it as their route to self-employment and financial independence. The road to gaining the prized green badge and licence is longer and harder than anywhere else in the world. To acquire the 'knowledge' means years spent travelling routes, memorizing roads and major buildings, and poring over detailed maps. The 'knowledge boys' are tested frequently by examiners who assess their ability to navigate the maze of London streets in their minds and imaginations. The desire to become financially independent means that aspiring London cabbies accept without question the need to internalize detailed maps and repeatedly practise journeys in their heads to achieve their desired objective.

How long is it since you stopped to consider the habits you have and the ones you would prefer not to have? The ones that are not good for your physical and mental well-being – too much smoking and drinking, always being late for appointments, nail biting, feeling depressed or being sarcastic and cynical. These subconscious habits which have been learned mostly by observation, but also by imitation and repetition, can be changed, through reversing the process. However, it is not possible to program your subconscious mind effectively to change a bad habit to a good one by giving it negative messages about how bad it is or your lack or will power.

When we train or practise for anything, we practise it repeatedly until it becomes second nature. Individuals who are lazy are practised at being lazy, while self-disciplined people are well practised in self-discipline. If you experience problems getting out of bed each morning at a certain time, as many people do, you will have to practise getting up when the alarm goes off. The more you practise the habit, the easier it will become. You should not be discouraged if it doesn't work every time; you are just out of practice, so you should repeat the exercise until it becomes a part of your life. The best way to get rid of bad habits is to work on replacing them one at a time with habits that are good for your mind and body. By visualizing yourself creatively as you would like to be and telling yourself how much better you will feel and setting realistic goals for achieving your aim, you can do it. Very few of the worthwhile things in life are easy to accomplish, so you should be patient and gentle with yourself – habits take time to acquire and time to dispose of successfully.

Relaxation, visualization, the creation of dream lists and goal-setting are valuable techniques to learn. They are also worth passing on to your children, even if they do not fully understand the nature of the sub-conscious image and the power of the dominant thought.

When my son Stephen was about ten years old, he started to show me pictures of BMX bicycles which were all the rage at the time. I told him that there was nothing wrong with the bicycle he had and I was not parting with money to buy a bicycle that didn't even have mudguards on it. Needless to say, he talked continually for weeks about getting a BMX bicycle and, in a moment of weakness, I asked him what model he would like to have if he ever had one, which he wasn't about to. He then told me that he wanted one built to his own specifications and had a complete list of the parts required to build it, which he enthusiastically showed me. He assured me that the nice man at the bicycle shop would put it all together for half as much again as the cost of a conventional racing bicycle. When I rebuffed this approach, he reminded me that I had told him that if he dreamt in detail long enough, then he could have anything he wanted. The situation was getting out of hand, so I told him that children had to get parental approval for their dream lists in advance. Trying to wriggle out of the situation as parents often do and trying to put him off, I told him that if he came to work in our business for an hour every morning before going to school, I would pay him so much a week. Well, he did come to work conscientiously every morning and, with some birthday money added to his savings, six months later we went to pick up his new bicycle. He derived years of pleasure riding and caring for his BMX bicycle and eventually sold it for 80 per cent of the original cost.

If you think that I was hard on my ten-year-old son, it is worth remembering that statistics show that a young person's first car is less likely to be involved in an accident and will last considerably longer if they buy it with their own money rather than one paid for by their parents. The quicker that children understand the relationship between their own efforts and the things they want in life, the better it is for them and their parents.

The reason that most people are unable to achieve their goals in life is that they do not define them sufficiently, do not learn enough about them and do not believe in them sufficiently to make them happen. We should live our lives with a sense of purpose, knowing where we plan to be standing in the future. We should understand that if we are not prepared to stand up for something in our lives today, we will be more likely to fall for anything in the future.

6

COMMUNICATION

When we meet someone for the first time, it takes approximately four minutes to decide whether we like or dislike each other. Statistics show that our decision will be based on the following criteria: on what we see, 87 per cent; hear, 7 per cent; smell, 3.5 per cent; touch, 1.5 per cent; and taste, 1 per cent. Some 55 per cent of people respond to body language, 38 per cent to the sound of a person's voice, and only 7 per cent to what a person says. It also seems that the average attention span has dropped to between 7 and 11 minutes. This is probably due to the influence of television – after a short while we lose concentration and anticipate a commercial break. Most people speak at a rate of 150 words a minute, but think at a rate of 600 words a minute. It is not surprising, therefore, that our minds tend to wander into a world of their own.

The quiet achievers know that the ability to communicate effectively internally with positive self-talk and externally with other people enables them to shape their world actively as they would like it to be. Good communication skills are essential for sharing ideas and experiences, and for explaining what it is you really want from other people. The successful transfer of information from one person to another assumes that both minds are operating at the same frequency and are on the same wavelength. We need to remember that the transmitter and receiver are different people who may view the world differently from each other. The right atmosphere of mutual interest and honesty sets the tone for meaningful communication to take place. One way to improve our own skills is to look closely at what good communicators actually do to get their messages across successfully to others:

- They know precisely what they want to convey to others.
- They know how to gain the attention of other people.
- They communicate at the level of the listeners' understanding.
- They choose the appropriate time and place to communicate.
- They give clear, concise and simple messages.
- They practise active listening and clarify the messages received.
- They stick to the point and are not easily distracted.
- They create trust by talking openly and honestly about themselves.

Many poor communicators have a problem expressing ideas that are different from those of others for fear of being rejected. They may also assume that other people automatically understand what they are saying, leaving their listeners to work out what they really meant. They are not willing to learn from others and may become frustrated, confused and isolated as a result. They may feel ignored and resentful, which causes them to experience difficulties in coping with everyday situations. Many young people today have been brought up in a more permissive environment, reject authority and want more say in decisions that may affect them personally. We all have a natural tendency to prefer people who show a genuine interest in our personal growth and development, who are people- rather than task-orientated. It is reassuring to note that, apart from speaking, listening, reading, writing and thinking, most top executives do practically nothing except communicate for their salaries.

Communication and financial skills are the best preparation for success in both the business and personal areas of life. Regardless of a person's occupation, good talkers tend to experience more success in every field of human endeavour.

Beyond our basic ability to communicate information, there are two aspects of the communication process – empathy and love – which we should consider further. We show empathy when we become more sensitive to the needs and differences of others rather than to our own concerns. The American Indians have a saying that we should walk a mile in another person's shoes if we would like to know them better.

People who are more successful tend to look at and think in terms of relative rather than absolute points of view. The groundwork to achieving more empathy lies in our awareness that each person is born equal in the real sense of the word, and that each person has an equal right to seek the fulfilment of their individual creative potential. Furthermore, we need to accept that the measure of a person's worth has nothing to do with their skin colour, country of origin or their political and religious beliefs, and that their value is not to be judged by their gender, financial position or their IQ. The road to real communication starts with the understanding that we are all distinct individuals with something special to contribute to the world around us.

A person is empathic when they understand that in a train each passenger may have different views and be seeing different things from where they happen to be seated. A person new to the journey may be watching the glimpses of natural scenery with real interest and delight. Someone else might be looking at the derelict buildings and contemplating the possibility of redeveloping them as a leisure centre. Another may have his head deep in a textbook, studying hard for a forthcoming examination, and be too engrossed to notice the scenery flashing by. Then again, someone else may be staring blankly out of the window, their mind fully occupied with trying to find solutions to pressing personal problems at home. It is important to take the time and to make the effort to see the world as others may see it, instead of assuming that they see it the same way that we do.

One way to develop more empathy is to become good finders, consciously looking for things to admire in others and praising them sincerely. There is good in everyone, however different their appearance, beliefs and life-style may be from our own. Simply by looking for that which is good in others, you are consciously communicating a message of loving acceptance. This is the message that we all want to receive most from others.

We all have prejudices about something and certain people that we carry around with us like so much excess baggage. I knew someone who had a dislike of men with beards and would never give them a position in his company. Another individual had an intense aversion to any woman who had red hair and would avoid them vigorously. The word prejudice means to judge beforehand or to form an unfavourable opinion before knowledge, thought or reason. We can only assume that the two individuals mentioned had had a bad experience with people who happened to have a certain appearance. This reduced the ability of the two individuals to get along with people with a similar appearance because they were unable to trust them.

We can also be prejudiced against people who we feel control the country, have all the money or are more successful than we are. We should check the validity of our prejudices by investigating them, and if we discover that they have no factual basis, reject them. We should not erect irrational barriers to communication through prejudices that lack substance or truth.

Furthermore, we should not repeat the prejudices of others which we do not know to be true; rather, we should check them before we voice an opinion. We know that if we repeat unproved stories about other people, they may return to us like unwelcome boomerangs. The one sure cure for prejudices is education because in the face of knowledge they disappear like drops of water on a hot stove. The reality is that while prejudice may cause pain and suffering to others, the person they hurt most in the long run is the one who holds them.

Real love, like self-esteem, is about independence and sharing ourselves with others, not out of need but through choice. Love is a relationship formed by two individuals who are capable of living free, self-sustaining and independent lives. Only those who are free and independent can really choose to enter and remain in a relationship. Dependent individuals enter and remain in a relationship out of necessity, not through choice. Relationships formed primarily from the physical attractiveness of the individuals concerned may lead to problems in the future. Furthermore, it is a poor individual who is unable to care about people other than their own family or friends because even animals and birds will do that much. We strive to expand the circle of our love and compassion to include all the people we come into contact with on a daily basis. Love is about listening attentively to what the other person is trying to say to us. We should overlook the imagined failings of other people in favour of looking for the good in them. We should tell people what it is we really like about them and how good it makes us feel whenever they are around. We should also make a real effort to stay in touch with family, friends and those we care about by visiting, writing and telephoning them often to let them know how much we appreciate them. We should understand that keeping in touch and being in touch is the secret to maintaining loving relationships.

When we meet someone new, we should extend our hands first as it is a time-honoured way for faithfully showing value to others. We should give a firm hand-shake, make direct eye contact and put a warm smile on our faces to show that we really are glad to meet them. We should say good morning or good afternoon, then offer them our names; we should do the same when we answer the telephone. We should make a sincere effort to listen actively to what the other person is saying by practising empathy. Finally, we should take note that talkers learn very little, while listeners learn a great deal.

Good communication also involves

• being comfortable and at ease when talking to strangers, and listening to them with open-minded interest. We should recall that all our existing friends were strangers once, so we should regard strangers as the friends we have yet to make.

- treating everyone we meet as an equal, even if their ideas and opinions do not agree with ours. We should listen with equal care to those who appear uneducated or boring, for everybody has their story to tell and is entitled to our full attention.
- asking people open-ended questions to draw them out and to show our interest in putting them at their ease
- not prying, but looking for special qualities in people that we can praise honestly and sincerely.
- striving to be pleasant and easy to understand by suiting the other person's style and pace.
- making people feel valued and appreciated and encouraged to do more.

  We should remember the times when we were young and people took the time to show a real interest and appreciation in us and our efforts, for example the teacher, minister or youth leader who encouraged and inspired us to do more with our lives through a genuine belief in our capabilities or the top people in our profession or career who have taken the time to show that they care about us by praising specific tasks we have managed to accomplish, however small they may have been in the larger scheme of things. It is very frustrating and demotivating when someone puts their best effort into achieving something that is of special value to them, anticipating the appreciation of others, only to find themselves ignored
- not making presumptions about what other people's responses may be to what we wish to say and neither should we attempt to read their minds.

The main reason for our self-assurance in meeting new

people is because we know that most individuals are eager to meet and become acquainted with others. We should be aware that however self-assured other people may appear, they are usually keen to make new friendships or personal contacts who may assist them to make more of their own lives. It is perfectly normal behaviour for new acquaintances to harbour a slight fear of being rejected or exploited by others. When we meet potential new friends, colleagues or members of our family group, we should adopt an attitude of service to them rather than considering our own self-interest.

We should always have other people's interests foremost in our minds when we communicate with them and there is an excellent reason for doing so. We all have the natural ability to read and sense each other's visual signals which are then interpreted by the subconscious mind. We instinctively warm to people who we sense are genuinely interested in what we are trying to tell them, even if we are unable to say precisely why it is we feel that way. We feel distinctly uneasy with people who appear to have their own interests uppermost in their minds, even if it is not obvious from what they are actually saying. This unspoken communication leads us to the feeling that what they are as a person is more important than what they may be trying to tell us. This feeling also leads us to question the value and worth of whatever it is they may be trying to communicate.

We may lie with our tongues but our bodies act in a distinct and revealing way, so the other person clearly perceives the real nature of our feelings. It seems that some people are always trying to force their ideas and impose their opinions on others for their own purposes. These people are generally surprised when others resist the strength of their carefully worded arguments and show resentment at being approached in this manner. The quiet achievers are open and honest in communicating their ideas, which invites mutual participation and generates useful feedback. They know that genuine warmth, friendliness and a gentle touch are the right attitude for real communication to take place.

7

FAITH

Without doubt, one of the most powerful principles that quiet achievers seem to possess in abundance is faith. We have all read about, heard of and seen stories in which ordinary people have accomplished things which at first glance seem impossible – for example, members of the emergency services who rescue people from burning buildings and crashed cars, and others who are plucked to safety from boats, aeroplanes or trains. There are stories of parents and grandparents who lift incredibly heavy objects to free trapped children, and of people who are sick or disabled supporting collapsing roofs or lifting cars, risking their own lives to save others. As a result of these near-miraculous feats of strength and physical endurance, these heroes and heroines become the subject of media attention. They usually appear somewhat embarrassed and bashful when they try to explain how they managed to accomplish these rescues. They say there was no one else to help them so they did what they had to do. The reality is that they were confronted with an unavoidable situation which required instant action. With no time to rationalize the situation or to procrastinate, they mobilized the innate power of faith which, for a limited time, suspended physical laws, enabling them to become superhuman beings.

Personally, I had difficulty in accepting the stories I read and saw on television regarding this kind of incident or I thought that they were highly exaggerated. This was particularly true if the stories appeared in certain sections of the media that rarely allow facts to stand in the way of a good story. Despite some initial scepticism, I made it a practice over several years to investigate the evidence to establish the validity of several incidents of this kind.

This has led me to become a real believer in the powerful energy of faith and what it can do for each of us. The late Carl Jung, a noted psychologist, observed that the human mind at deeper levels has a need to recognize that a superhuman element exists. Avowed atheists may see this need as irrational psychological nonsense, but even they have been known to call upon some unseen power for assistance or comfort during an emergency or personal crisis. Many psychologists, including Jung, have noticed that those who hold traditional or transcendental philosophies of life generally cope better with the inevitable stresses and strains of modern living. It seems that the quiet achievers recognize the empowering nature of faith and see it as being of primary importance in the achievement of any meaningful success. The absence of faith prevents many people from experiencing any significant growth or success in their lives. Faith as a positive power brings into physical reality that which we hope for but which is as yet unseen. In this context, it is worth remembering that the true meaning of the word hope is not vague wishful-thinking, but joyful expectation.

Faith can be likened to the electricity in our homes. No

one really knows what electricity is, but we all know what it can be used for. Power stations constantly try to match supply with the demands placed on them as any excess energy is simply wasted. Electricity is conducted through insulated cables in our homes where we control the switches that put it to good use in our lives. When we turn on the lights in our homes we really expect them to come on, not vaguely wish that they would do so.

Some people know as little about the power of electricity as they do about the power of faith. I remember pulling over in my car once to talk to a friend who was an overhead linesman who had just cut out a large section of power cable between two pylons. I walked over to examine the cable and a bystander yelled out to me, 'Don't touch that cable.' When I asked why not, he said, 'There might still be some electricity left in it.' I can only assume that the person also believed that there was more electricity at the bottom of the curve in the cable between the pylons because it somehow naturally collected there!

The difference between wishing and expecting is important to understand, as it is a key factor to being successful. If you wished that you had a certain amount of money in your bank account, you would not write a cheque on that particular account. On the other hand, if you expected to have that amount in your bank account by a specified date, you could confidently write a cheque on that account. Some people wish that their problems in life would go away. We expect that they will and the solution to the problem is already on its way. There is never an absence of faith; it is always available if we want to put it to work on our behalf. Some people mobilize its negative counterpart which gives them premonitions of their most deeply held fears, leading them to lose hope of making any progress.

Down the ages, wise people, philosophers and enlightened scientific minds have discussed the validity of the self-fulfilling prophecy. They have examined how the power of the self-fulfilling prophecy might affect the future of individuals and of countries. The theory is that our assumptions about any situation dictate our behaviour towards others. Other people then make assumptions about our behaviour towards them, which in turn dictate their behaviour towards us. This leads us to conclusions about them, which starts the cycle all over again. The latest thinking of the self-fulfilling prophecy appears to be that it is neither true nor false, but that is is capable of becoming true of an individual or nation if they believe in it.

We learned previously that our minds are unable to distinguish between a real-life experience and one that is vividly and repeatedly imagined. We should appreciate the importance of the dual concepts of faith and belief as powerful allies in realizing our own creative potential. All our lives are self-fulfilling prophecies in the sense that we may not necessarily get what we want, but we will generally get what we expect.

A great deal remains undiscovered about the precise way in which our thoughts can and do influence our emotional states, which then affect our physical bodies. A significant body of medical opinion does accept that there is a direct correspondence between psyche and soma, or mind and body. The thoughts and preoccupations of the mind become moving forces that cause positive or negative effects on the general stability or harmony of our bodily functions. What the mind harbours, the body will manifest to mirror our past and current thinking about any situation.

The quiet achievers who have a positive 'can do, want

to' outlook on life are motivated by the rewards of success and generate a lesser known form of stress called
eustress. Eustress is a word that was coined by the late Dr
Hans Selye, a pioneer in stress research, to describe the
positive aspects of stress. Eustress gives them a feeling of
more energy and personal power accompanied by an
overall sense of well-being. Their counterparts who have
a negative 'can't do, won't do' outlook are motivated by
the penalties of failure and generate the better known
form of stress called distress. Distress gives them feelings
of discomfort, anxiety, disorientation and ill health.

If a parent heard that a son or daughter was missing,
believed dead, in a plane crash in a remote region, they
would show the characteristic symptoms of distress.
They would not be able to relax or sleep properly,
their hormone levels would begin to fall, their stomach
linings would start to dissolve and they would lose their
appetites. If, some months later, they were told that
their son or daughter had miraculously survived the
crash and was alive and well, having been found by
friendly natives, the feelings of joy, happiness and a
sense of tremendous relief they would experience are
known as 'eustress'. The physical symptoms created by
both lots of news were not caused by what actually
happened, but by the state of mind or attitude that
produced the different physical results.

One of the basic survival instincts we have carried
over from earliest times is our finely tuned fight or flight
mechanism. This was very useful if a sabre-toothed tiger
leapt out of the bushes to devour a passing human. This
instinctive behaviour enabled primitive people to distinguish in a split second whether it really was a tiger or
simply a friendly neighbour coming through the bushes.
Nowadays, too many people act as if they are facing

life-threatening situations every day when in fact they
are not. We all have a fixed deposit in our distress
accounts on which we can draw, and if we make too
many withdrawals we will age faster and die sooner as a
consequence of our own attitude to life. We should prefer to draw on our limitless eustress accounts which will
help us to stay younger, live longer and lead productive,
healthy lives. If we become overly worried, anxious or
fearful regarding some real or imagined situations, we
will experience the effects of distress.

Distress has a direct effect on our endocrine system
which produces the hormones and antibodies which pro-
tect our natural immune defence system. When our
immune defence system barriers are lowered by distress,
this reduces our resistance to many common ailments.
We are then more susceptible to the environmental haz-
ards, bacteria and viruses which are always present to a
larger or smaller degree in our physical surroundings.
The consequences of being distressed can lead to
physical illness as a direct result of our own thinking
processes. The medical profession has long recognized
that our past or current thinking does have a profound
effect on our ability to respond to any course of medical
treatment. It also stands to reason that a positive mental
attitude is a definite ally in the body's healing process,
regardless of a person's age or condition.

An 87-year-old lady was knocked down by a car while
crossing a road near a retirement village. She sustained
multiple injuries and the woman driver of the car who
waited with her for the ambulance to arrive was
understandably distraught by what had happened. The
badly injured elderly lady, despite agonizing pain,
comforted and reassured the woman driver who had
knocked her down. In hospital, the accident victim

had emergency surgery performed by an orthopaedic surgeon who was amazed that she survived the operation as she had a weak heart. She was told that she would have to spend the rest of her life in a wheelchair, which this previously active lady could not accept. Being persistent, she asked what it would take to make her mobile again. She was told that she would need at least two further major orthopaedic operations and several skin grafts, which she was not likely to survive given her heart condition and age. Determined to regain her former mobility, however, she insisted against all the best advice available to undergo the necessary operations.

During her seven-month-stay in hospital, the old lady amazed staff and patients alike by her cheerfulness. When talking to his colleagues, the surgeon called her his 'miracle lady'. Finally, the day came when she was released from hospital with a walking frame. She received meals and cleaning help at home on a daily basis. Within four weeks, she dispensed with her home helps and meals, and the walking frame was exchanged for two walking-sticks. Three months later, walking without assistance, she was asked by neighbours how she had managed to cope with her ordeal. The lady replied to the effect that she had never believed in putting her wishbone where her backbone ought to be. She had many other pearls of wisdom which she lived by and shared with family and friends. This remarkable woman is now a lively 94 years young, and has always been a source of inspiration and encouragement by example to me, her son.

Our hormones play an important part in regulating biological functions. Adrenaline enables us to fight or flee in response to imminent danger or to respond to calls for superhuman effort. Insulin regulates the level of various sugars in the bloodstream. Scientists discovered about 30 years ago the existence of several morphine-like substances called endorphins and enkephalins. These natural substances which we produce in our bodies not only block pain but also give us a natural lift or feeling of well-being. Endorphins help to control the brain's perception of pain and stress, and form part of the body's natural pain-relieving system. Research chemists have created artificial endorphin and studied its therapeutic use in relieving severe pain. Although these substances occur naturally in the body, producing only beneficial effects, they cause dependence when administered as a drug.

Our own thinking processes can cause our bodies to produce enough adrenaline to perform superhuman feats of strength. We can also produce natural pain-relievers that are from 50 to 100 times more powerful than morphine that give us a natural feeling of elation. Is it not also possible, therefore, for us to harness this demonstrable, practical power of faith in action in our bodies and put it to good use in our daily lives?

The quiet achievers know that this is true and, unlike artificially produced substances, the only side-effect of this kind of treatment is more happiness. Through the daily use of positive words of power such people see what they believe in with conviction coming into reality. The self-destructive talk of negative people leads them to believe only in the things that they can see here and now, and to generate more negativity. When people ask why you are so optimistic and cheerful all the time, you can reply that you are on a new drug called endorphin. They will probably answer knowingly that they thought you must be on something, as it is unnatural to be so happy all the time.

To cultivate more faith and optimism in our lives we should spend more time with cheerful optimists than with the doom-and-gloom crowd. Let us become more familiar with the solution-orientated pair, optimism and realism, than with the problem-orientated couple, pessimism and cynicism. We all know people who say that they are sicker than we are, and that their partner is worse, their children more ungrateful and their job worse than ours. If we were to tell these people that by constantly repeating these fables they are actually maintaining their world that way, they would think that we had taken leave of our senses.

Some people change partners for someone who turns out to be similar in many respects to their former partner. They will change jobs often, only to encounter the same difficulties that they experienced with previous employers. Some individuals even change countries in the hope that a new environment will prove more favourable to them, only to find similar difficulties to the ones they had before. Many people will change partners, jobs and countries instead of accepting that all worthwhile change begins with them. It seems that they face the same problems over and over again, until they learn a personal lesson which will enable them to make progress. They can travel the world over only to find themselves back at the place from which they started, with themselves.

We can seek to develop a circle of people around us where the attraction is in our mutual values and goals, not in sharing needs and problems. If we find ourselves becoming depressed, we can consider the plight of those who are less fortunate than ourselves throughout the world and count our blessings. If that does not work, we can take a more positive view by taking a walk and watching children playing in a park or beside a river to regain a sense of proportion in our life. A change of scenery by visiting the seaside or the country is often enough to change our outlook on life for the better. We can choose to listen to inspiring music which gives our spirits a lift, rather than to depressing sounds which lower our emotional tone. A wise man once said that music soothes the savage breast. The other side of the coin may be that certain music can turn us into savage beasts. Interesting research has been carried out in the field of subliminal learning whereby barely audible spoken information is overlaid with music, the listener being unaware of anything except the pleasant sounds. It appears that the choice of music makes a real difference in the effectiveness of this accelerated subliminal learning technique. Music with a gentler beat and tone appears to open up the creative right side of the brain while enhancing the ability to absorb the information.

We can make a habit of reading quality newspapers for important and useful information, resisting the temptation to read the sordid scandal about other people's lives or to dwell on depressing tragedies. The media appear to operate on a philosophy that bad news sells, but this news is rarely a true reflection of the world that we really inhabit. By concentrating on what is worst in people, the media transmit a feeling of self-satisfaction to some. If the media featured the quiet achievers more, it would act as a challenge to less positive individuals to do more. Perhaps they would spend less time as 'couch potatoes' sitting in front of their televisions and spend more time with optimists and activities with those they love. Instead of complaining about what a hard day it has been or questioning why someone doesn't take action over a particular issue, or why God has picked on them again with a problem, perhaps they could try saying what a really active day they have had and that they are looking forward to some worthwhile recreational pastimes. We will get high on our own creative imaginations by visualizing what it will feel like when we attain the goals we have set for ourselves and get those endorphins working on our behalf.

Positive educational and recreational activities, quality magazines and television programmes that specialize in the wonders of nature or are culturally stimulating can help us in our quest for faith. We can choose films and videos for their quality and story value rather than for their commercial appeal or emphasis on the less desirable human characteristics. We can think, speak and visualize ourselves as being in good health every day and avoid dwelling on minor physical ailments. If we pay too much attention to coughs, colds and other minor illnesses, they will repay our kind attention by becoming some of our best friends who will frequently visit us.

We should take the time to demonstrate our faith in practical ways by passing it to others who may need theirs topping up from time to time. We can do this by telephoning, visiting or writing regularly to someone in need to show that we really care about them and we should endeavour to do this every day of our lives.

8

ADAPTABILITY

Adaptability is the hallmark of the quiet achievers who are to be found in every walk of life. For many people, this is a worrying period in history as they bide their time hoping that the future will offer brighter prospects for them to put their plans and dreams into action. Some people would prefer to return to the good old days when a haircut cost 50p and a good night out on the town cost less than £5. It was a time when you had job security for life, and life was altogether more simple and uncomplicated. People were kinder, the air was fresher and cleaner, there was less crime and life was generally more enjoyable in the good old days. If we picked up a newspaper today and turned to the editorial column, we would not be surprised to read something along the following lines:

> The world is too big for us – too much going on, too much crime, too much violence. Try as you will, you always seem to be behind in the race, it is an incessant strain just to keep pace without losing ground. Science pours its discoveries on you so fast you stagger with hopeless bewilderment. Everything is high pressure and human nature cannot endure much more.

This message is typical of the view held by many people regarding the current state of affairs in world history. It is an interesting fact that this particular newspaper editorial actually appeared over 160 years ago in 1833. So what does this really mean to each of us living in the 1990s? I believe that it teaches us a valuable lesson which we need to appreciate fully to enable us to make the most of our lives.

Our minds have a natural tendency to forget most of the bad things about the past and to recall only the pleasant memories. By looking back through rose-coloured glasses, we fail to appreciate that the good old days are really here and now. A primary reason for this lack of appreciation is that far too many people concentrate on their current problems and prefer to imagine all the good times they had in the past. Another reason why people appear to be unable to appreciate that the good old days are here now is that they have failed to learn from history that problems are always a normal part of everyday life. Perhaps people prefer to put the emphasis on how different things are today in an effort to justify their own lack of productivity and progress. It seems as if nothing is really new in today's world, with some things conveniently forgotten and other things fondly remembered. Each generation competes with the last in trying to prove that theirs is labouring under the most difficult and trying circumstances in the entire history of the human race. Through a combination of moaning, groaning and complaining about how tough things are, they feel free to hibernate in a cave of their own making until a day with brighter prospects dawns. Meanwhile, they manage to avoid the necessity of rolling up their sleeves and doing something creative about finding solutions to their own problems. They prefer to blame their lack of productivity on the older generation who have made such a mess of the world they inhabit. Some of the older generation prefer to blame the younger generation for being such an undisciplined, ungrateful and basically lazy group of people. The government is a popular target for everyone to blame for creating the conditions that prevent people from being able to make any progress in life. These people play their own particular version of the game 'hide and seek' in which everybody runs away to hide and somebody else is always 'It'. They are always looking for someone to give them a helping hand up or a free hand-out, instead of using the hands attached to their own arms.

Our responses to changes vary according to the speed at which they happen and how those changes may affect us personally. Gradual changes can occur – for example, the steady advance of a welfare state and the perception by 50 per cent of the people that they are actively supporting the other 50 per cent of the population. Our responses to change vary according to the speed at which they happen and how those changes may affect us personally. Gradual changes can and do occur without us being consciously aware of their cumulative effects.

For example, the improved reliability of cars means that they now need less servicing, provide better fuel consumption and have tyres that need changing less often. Television sets and other electrical goods are superior in performance and reliability by comparison with similar items produced 20 years ago. It may be equally true that there have been gradual and perceptible changes of a less desirable nature taking place in our society. Some people believe that our moral and ethical standards as individuals and as a nation are being steadily eroded. We need to be aware of all these changes taking place if we are going to respond or react to them in the most effective way as individuals.

Sudden changes such as stock market crashes or wars cause dramatic changes that have immediate effects around the world. Individuals may find themselves confronted by events which they may not have foreseen which require them to alter their approach to life dramatically. Changing our behaviour, learning new skills and adapting to altered circumstances can be a powerful means for transforming ourselves and even for gaining a competitive edge.

Maybe we need to learn from the chameleon, a creature which inhabits an ever-changing and potentially dangerous environment. A chameleon can exist without food for long periods while remaining alert to opportunities and is capable of making split-second decisions. Undoubtedly, the ability to blend with its surroundings by changing colour or character is the key which ensures the continued survival and prosperity of this adaptable creature. When it comes to adapting to inevitable or unforeseen changes in your life, how do you react?

Many individuals resist adapting to inevitable changes in their circumstances or do not see change as an opportunity for personal growth. They refer to familiar sayings such as, 'You can't teach an old dog new tricks' or 'A leopard never changes its spots' when they refuse to embrace the chance to take stock of their lives and to consider alternative pathways. They fail to recognize that the main difference between animals and humans lies in our ability to re-create ourselves as a matter of personal choice.

Some people, for example, change their lives through education. Mature students, some past the usual retiring age, return to colleges and universities to gain new qualifications either for profit or pleasure. Many have no prior exposure to higher education, having left the formal education system at an early age. They discover that the experience they have gained during their working lives gives them a natural advantage over their younger fellow students. This association with fresh young minds also stimulates them to consider a whole new range of previously forgotten possibilities for their own lives.

Some people choose to alter their life-styles dramatically in mid-life and to pursue a completely different course of action which leaves others shaking their heads in disbelief. Friends of mine in Australia owned a successful contract chemical manufacturing business that gave them and their three children an enviable material life-style. They sold it and moved out to the 'bush' 40 miles from the nearest town to a 50-acre plot of land that had no house on it, no electricity, gas, running water or sewerage. They lived in an old caravan while they cleared the land, built a house complete with solar-powered hot-water system and electricity-generating plant. They set up an extensive trickle-irrigation system fed with water from a small river to grow obscure varieties of organic vegetables which they sold through an agent to city restaurants. This relatively quiet alternative country life-style was in complete contrast to their hectic, conventional, city life. Their income was around 40 per cent of what it had been, but their expenditure had dropped dramatically to compensate for it. They now worked hard for just five months of the year, compared to the constant 84-hour weeks they were used to working in their former business. They had the time to pursue their real interests and to spend precious time with their children who had previously seen very little of their parents. They lived in clear, crisp mountain air instead of in a polluted and noisy city environment.

It was not an easy transformation for the family, as my friend Kelvin described it. It was

> like being in a short dark corridor with a door at each end and they are just far enough apart to prevent you keeping them both open at the same time. You have to let the one behind you close fully before you can move forwards and open the one in front of you. The worst part was being stuck in that dark corridor with both doors closed at once.

For some individuals it is not a matter of such dramatic changes of life-style. They may simply choose, in fact, to adapt their existing skills to a new opportunity which presents itself. For example, a successful disposable paper-products salesman in his 50s who had reached the limits of his personal job satisfaction was looking for a new challenge. One of his favourite sayings was, 'When you're green, you're growing; when you're ripe, you begin to rot.' During his travels, he was fascinated by two of his customers who were brothers. They ran a conventional take-away food business along unconventional lines, having successfully adapted the mass-production techniques of large factories to their small business operation with excellent results. The salesman clearly saw the possibilities that the wide-scale application of these methods opened up to someone who was prepared to accept the challenges involved. He borrowed heavily to finance his dream, gave up his secure well-paid job and threw himself into the task he had set himself. Ray Kroc was equal to the task and those familiar golden-arch entrances to McDonald's restaurants are tangible proof that it is never too late to start over again.

The quiet achievers realize that the best days of their lives are those of the present because now is the only time when they will have the opportunity to accomplish anything at all. They understand that even the wisest people do not know when they will be called upon to give an account of their actions on earth and to say that they were waiting for things to get better first will not be an acceptable answer. The quiet achievers live each day as if it were their last because they know that one day it *will* be. They plan their lives, however, as if they were going to live a thousand years. They have learned to take the small things in life seriously when they deal with others and to take the serious things in their own lives lightly. They regard adapting to change as a normal part of everyday living and consider problems to be natural minor inconveniences.

If we look back at the good old days without our rose-coloured glasses, we appreciate how truly fortunate we are to be living at this point in time. In the past, people suffered from the often fatal diseases of diphtheria, poliomyelitis, rubella, smallpox, cholera, typhoid fever and tuberculosis, just to mention a few. People had large families, only a percentage of whom survived to adulthood and some of those were crippled or disfigured for life. Death was a familiar visitor to even the richest households and the undertaker's hearse was an everyday sight. There was no running water, electricity, gas or indoor toilets. Saturday nights were special as it was bath night: the family shared the same water in order of seniority. It was really something to look forward to if you were the youngest of twelve children and your father happened to keep pigs for a living! A decent education was the privilege of the rich and leisured class, while the first thing that working-class people learned was how to tell the time so that they could turn up at the factory gates when needed. In the good old days, there was no spare money for insurance, health care, savings for old age or holidays.

Given the rapid pace of change, can we visualize what the future has in store for our children and grandchildren 30 or 40 years from now? It is quite possible that oil-based fuels like petrol and diesel will have given way to the newly emerging liquid hydrogen-powered engines that are being developed today. Fears of an impending shortage of fossil-based fuels may prove to be as unfounded as they were about diminishing supplies of whale oil in times past. Newspaper headlines announced: 'World to go dark due to shortage of whale blubber.' Such fears helped the development of gas and, later, electric lighting.

One of the major benefits of the liquid hydrogen-powered cars that our children will be driving is that they emit pure oxygen from their exhausts. Instead of creating pollution, these cars and similarly powered trucks and buses will be cruising our highways sucking up and filtering out pollution like environmentally friendly vacuum cleaners.

Schools will be used as community resource centres to promote the arts, sports, cultural activities and civic duties. There will be no classrooms, pupils or teachers as we know them today. The children of tomorrow will study at home using powerful multi-media computers connected to the worldwide Internet by optical cable telephone and by satellite dishes tuned to orbiting educational satellites. Students will be able to communicate directly with other learners from countries around the world using built-in electronic translators, the effect of which will help to promote mutual understanding, peace and goodwill.

Children will be given aptitude and personality tests

to enable them to choose the fields of study in which they are most likely to succeed by being themselves. This will lead them to follow careers where they will contribute further to society and be happier people, too. Their tutors will be non-critical and have endless patience in encouraging them to develop at their own pace in order to develop their full potential. Children will no longer become disinterested because they are held back by those who are slower than themselves; the slow learners will be encouraged to progress at their own pace without pressure. Learning will be fun and everyone will find that they can do well in some area of life. They will regard adult education as a pleasurable experience, to be taken up throughout their lives. Parents will tell their children that they do not know how fortunate they are and about the difficulties they experienced when they were young. They will tell them about the old-fashioned cars they drove that were powered by fuel made from oil which was frantically pumped out of the earth and sea until it ran out. They will also tell them how they had to get out of bed early and walk in all kinds of weather to a place known as a school. On arrival at school, they were all crowded into a small classroom where they had to study the same subjects at the same pace as everybody else, whether they liked it or not. They had to sit examinations in set subjects to progress to higher levels of education. These examinations led to professions that often had little to do with some of the subjects they had had to learn. They were excluded from occupations that they could have excelled at because only academic success counted – aptitude and personality did not carry weight.

The children of tomorrow will probably think how strange it must have been to have lived in such a quaint, backward world and they will probably assume that we are exaggerating just to make them feel grateful. The world they will inhabit will be taken for granted and some of them will have invented new excuses for sticking their heads in the sand, just as older generation did.

The younger generation is getting taller, stronger, healthier and smarter than at any other time in the history of the Western world. Young athletes are routinely breaking world records set in the 60s, 70s and 80s, and they are pushing back the frontiers of what seemed impossible a generation ago. Young entrepreneurs are creating new businesses by adapting faster to the needs of the younger generation than their more conservative competitors. The success of companies like Microsoft, Apple and Dell in the home and business computer fields shows their ability to achieve success in a rapidly changing world. Young people are travelling more than at any other time in history in search of new ideas, cultures and experiences. Many of them are adapting more traditional ways of life to our modern society which may appear unusual to some people, but in fact are part of a more open way of living.

Some young people are turning their backs on a predominantly materialistic life-style in favour of a way of life that requires fewer possessions, which is said to be a characteristic of the Aquarian era. In the year 2020 it will not be unusual for young students to take a school field-trip to Australia on Richard Branson's sub-orbital *Virgin Pacific* space shuttle. Australia, with its fabulous beaches and unique wildlife, will be a popular destination, taking around the same time to reach as the Eurostar train now takes to travel from Britain to Belgium via the channel tunnel, or Concorde takes to fly the Atlantic Ocean. No doubt the students will be able to telephone home on their digital satellite telephones to reassure their families that they are safely tucked up in their Sydney hotel rooms when they have, in fact, travelled across to Singapore for a night out on the town. Some things never really change over the years, and being a young adult is likely to remain one of them.

We need to recognize that the ability to adapt to our changing world involves acceptance of the fact that all change begins with our willingness to change ourselves. The ancient Chinese symbol or pictogram which symbolizes an impending crisis is identical with the one which means opportunity. The symbol can be interpreted as meaning 'Crisis is an opportunity riding the dangerous winds'. The quiet achievers believe this saying to mean that by adapting to change they view a crisis as an opportunity to learn and to grow. They see the stumbling blocks which we all encounter along the way as being convertible into stepping-stones that will assist them along the pathway towards their main goals in life.

When we are faced with unforeseen and potentially disruptive situations in our lives, we should respond by regarding them as minor inconveniences and not as major problems. We should have learned that to live well entails resolving the problems that are almost as common to many of us as breathing in and out. Many people fail to realize that they have far more problem-solving ability within them than they really appreciate.

The first stage to resolve any problem is to define it properly. If you have several problems confronting you, you should tackle them one at a time. Take the biggest problem first and sit down with a sheet of paper and write as detailed a description of it as you possibly can. The simple act of spelling it out in detail often minimizes the size of the problem, as we tend to fear that which we are unable to see clearly. The next step is to divide the problem into specific factual details, leaving out opinions so that the problem is as real as you think it is. Then write down as many possible solutions that come into your mind, including those which at first glance may appear ridiculous. Try talking the problem through with someone you know and trust whose opinions you have learnt to value. If this fails to produce a satisfactory solution, start to gather as much information as possible that may have a bearing on the matter which concerns you. You should know and accept that a solution to the problem exists and that you are perfectly capable of finding it.

Before you go to bed at night, review all the information you have acquired, then simply relax and let your subconscious mind go to work on the problem while you sleep. Your subconscious mind rivals the most powerful computers ever built with regard to problem-solving and it will get to work on finding a solution while you enjoy a good night's rest. Plan to get up half-an-hour earlier than usual, make yourself a warm drink, sit down quietly with pen and paper, and write down any solutions that surface in your conscious mind. The answer will appear then or later when you least expect it – in the shower, when you are driving to work or when you are simply sitting around doing nothing in particular. The answers have a tendency to slip into our conscious minds unannounced and seem to be right immediately. Often the solution appears to be so straightforward and obvious in hindsight, that you may wonder why you did not manage to think of it before.

Quiet achievers think of problems as normal occurrences that are simply awaiting an appropriate solution. They do not worry unduly about or fear problems as this would only cause them sleepness nights. They know that by facing up to their problems and making a real effort to solve them effectively, the answers will always be forth-coming. We should also remember that in adapting to the changing circumstances of our lives, it is of fundamental importance to treat the serious matters lightly and to take the light matters seriously.

9

≺≋≻

DETERMINATION

Do you know someone who appears to have an unlimited supply of energy for all the things they do in life and wondered where they get all that energy from? Some people appear to accomplish so much in a relatively short space of time, but how do they manage to do that?

For quiet achievers the answer appears to be related to the amount of determination and enthusiasm they bring to all the things they do in life. The amount of energy we are willing to use in accomplishing any task is directly connected to how much we really want to achieve a particular goal or to gain a particular reward. Try as we might, it is simply not possible to create any more energy from within ourselves. We are all born with a given amount of energy and we can only choose to liberate or transform the energy we already have in our possession. Those individuals who seem to be lacking in energy all the time are simply storing theirs up for the future. Our determination to accomplish any task with enthusiasm raises our energy levels to perform the desired action or task.

When we anticipate an evening out with good friends even though we may have had a laborious and tiring day at work, we can still be full of energy. Normally after a hard day, we might have been content to relax and unwind into our favourite easy chair and read a newspaper or watch television. If we lack real energy when it relates to our work, perhaps it is worth reconsidering what it is we are actually working for now and towards in the future. A professional landscape gardener may prefer to go deep-sea fishing at the weekends, while a professional fisherman might choose to spend his leisure hours working in his garden.

People wrongly assume that people in the higher income professions such as medicine and law are somehow immune from feeling that they would like to do something different with their lives. Many well-educated individuals bow to family pressure to follow a family tradition instead of pursuing a career that is more suited to their aptitude, personality or real interests. Others feel obliged by the sacrifices of their parents to be what their parents would have liked to have been themselves. Some discover after years of hard study and training for a particular occupation that it is too late to go back to the starting line and go down an entirely different track. Very often well-paid professional, competent and apparently successful individuals who are held in high regard by the community, would prefer to be doing something else for a living.

Most quiet achievers tend to regard their careers as being pleasurable and enjoyable activities that they look forward to pursuing each day. People with a more negative attitude tend to regard their work as a form of prison sentence to be endured until they are paroled at the weekends or for their holidays when they can do what they really want to.

Most people are about as happy as they make up their

minds to be in any occupation, and it is worth noting that cheerful optimists generally earn more than gloomy pessimists. Quiet achievers do not automatically bounce out of bed each day full of the joys of living, but they have discovered that if they act enthusiastically at the start of each day, they will quickly become enthusiastic. They realize that occasionally their minds are not assisting them to be happy, but by acting happy anyway their minds soon follow suit.

The young person who after school may look as if he or she will fail to walk up the road to reach home and who collapses in front of the television set exhausted, is not the same young person who, on reaching home, knows that he or she is ready to go out on a date later that evening. Our enthusiastic determination to accomplish anything in life taps the supplies of energy available within ourselves and withdraws the right amount to accomplish the task. The stronger the determination and the bigger the purpose, the more energy we can summon up to meet those demands. To be full of energy, the quiet achievers find something to work towards that is always just out of their grasp and slightly beyond their present capabilities. Their determination to do better than their previous best, challenges and interests them to the point where they begrudge the sleep that takes them away from the pursuit of these goals.

We hear so much about success in all areas of life that we tend to lose sight of the fact that the right to fail is as important as the right to succeed. We have all failed so many times that we may have difficulty in remembering some of the occasions because they seem so long ago. How many times did we fall down when we were trying to walk? How often did we fall off our bicycles while we were learning to ride them? The first time that we tried to swim, many of us came perilously close to drowning and few of us were instant sports champions when it came to learning new games. How many thousands of ways did Thomas Edison find not to make a functioning electric light-bulb and how long did it take Albert Einstein to gain grudging acceptance for his theory of relativity? How many rejection slips did some of our most popular and talented authors receive before they were accepted and how many good speakers were bad speakers when they first started out?

We need to appreciate the fact that virtually nothing worthwhile works first time – it is always a matter of doing it, fixing it and trying it again. Quiet achievers do not worry about their past failures. However, they do seriously worry about the chances that they may miss out on if they don't even try something new.

The British love complaining about the weather – it is one of our national pastimes – but how often do they stop to consider that if there were no bad weather, they would be unable to appreciate fully the good weather? How many of us really appreciate being fit and healthy until an accident or illness puts us out of action for a while? It is a rare individual whose success was not crucially influenced by some kind of prior failure. Unpopular as it may be these days, the fact remains that it is impossible to achieve any meaningful success without some form of personal sacrifice and effort. If you personally have not made the sacrifice and effort, then someone else has probably made them for you. If you are making the sacrifice and effort now, it may be so that someone else may succeed after you or that you will experience success later on.

Any form of success has to be earned by following a

determined course of action for a calculated length of time. We should realize that any worthwhile achievement is impossible if it requires no effort, because success is a process of natural selection whereby only those who keep trying will eventually achieve their goal. Successful individuals see failures as temporary setbacks that make them determined to adapt and change their approach to the problems they encounter. They refuse to stay down for long or to be excessively hard on themselves because they realize that it is a waste of time and valuable energy. They know that they will eventually break through the barrier to achieve their reward if they simply persevere for long enough. Many successful people recall the times when just as they were about to reach their goal, they suffered a setback and found themselves at the starting post again. It is like the salmon which must forge their way upstream against the flow, only to be swept downstream repeatedly before they eventually reach the spawning grounds in the higher reaches of the river. The truth is that we have to push on through the tough times to experience those real break throughs in our lives.

First-class athletes push their bodies to the point where they feel that they can do no more. Their lungs feel as if they would burst and the painful cramp in their legs and thighs sends urgent messages to their brains which declare: 'That's it, I can't go any further or faster. I've had enough.' This is known as 'hitting the wall'. Seasoned athletes know that 'the wall' is not the end – it's a signal that they are on the verge of a break-through. They toughen up and push themselves though the wall and gain a valuable second wind. They go faster than before, reaching levels of excellence that can only be attained in this way. This is known as gaining the winner's edge.

When you feel at your worst and that failure is

breathing down your neck, this is the time to press on as never before. Then, quite suddenly, like the dawning of a new day, light will pour in and you will see the way to make a break-through. All you need to do is to punch one tiny hole in the wall and to keep enlarging that hole to demolish every obstacle which may be standing in your way. Once you have had that kind of life-changing experience, you will never be the same again. A single break-through will turn you into a never-say-die champion. Only those individuals with a clear sense of purpose, faith and determination manage to scale the heights to achieve the really big goals in life.

This does not mean that individuals with less exalted goals or ambitions in life are failures – that is far from the truth. Everyone is a success in their own way if they have achieved what they truly want in life and are content – it all comes down to a matter of individual choice. Anyone may experience success if they are willing to pay the price tag attached to it, but real success hinges on being yourself and having the ability to enjoy paying the price every day.

We may not all become millionaires or media stars, but we can all experience more success, whether it be in our careers, personal life or in other areas of our lives. The administration assistant can become the head of a section, a salesperson can become the area manager and a shop assistant can own his or her own business. Someone looking after children at home can study to return to work in a better position than one formerly held and the amateur sportsperson can practise to perform as a professional in the future. The price which you should enjoy paying is seen as a continuing process, otherwise you may slip backwards should you decide to rest on your current achievements.

Quiet achievers are not workaholics. They plan on spending valuable time with their family and friends and for quiet periods to work on their own personal growth. Many well-meaning parents devote far too much time and energy pursuing material rewards to bestow on their children and may be highly regarded as good providers by their acquaintances. In later years, however, when the children have grown up and moved away from home, parents often complain that their offspring fail to see them as often as they would like. They say that they gave their children every material advantage in life, but they fail to realize until it is too late that the most valuable gift that children need from their parents is their time.

We all need to define what success really means to each of us in every area of our lives, not just that portion of time we allocate to our careers. We should then decide how much time we are prepared to spend thinking about and working towards the separate goals we have set ourselves in these areas. We should recognize that this is an ongoing process which we should consult our partners about regularly to enlist their active co-operation and support. We should accept that when the going gets tough and we experience temporary setbacks, our determination to achieve our heart's desire will help us to reach our goal. Life was not meant to be easy and only those individuals whose dreams are greater than the thought of the work involved in making them a reality ever achieve greatness.

Quiet achievers tend to be dreamers who have found a dream too exciting and important for it to remain a fantasy. Determination is really the test of faith, when it becomes hard to stay focused on that flickering light at the end of a long dark tunnel, even when they know that they are doing the right thing.

A significant attribute of the more successful individuals in our society is their belief in an all-embracing power which is responsible for the creation and maintenance of the universe that we all inhabit. They believe in a perpetual promise of abundant prosperity to those who are determined to keep moving forward even when they have nothing but their dreams to hang on to. When circumstances hinder their progress in the outer world, they turn within themselves to nurture their inner vision of the way things will be in the near future. Quiet achievers use their creative imaginations to visualize their goals and maintain an abiding faith in their convictions which allows them to bend and spring back when faced with the inevitable winds of change. The ability to bend and bounce back is reflected in the way that they can always manage to see the brighter side to even the gloomiest of prospects. When faced with the fiercest winds they remain calm, relaxed and centred in the eye of life's storms because, as incurable optimists, they know that it is an ill wind that does not benefit someone, somewhere in the world.

Why does successful living appear to be an elusive mystery to so many people when everyone says they want it so much? People buy countless books which promise access to secrets which will somehow magically transform them into millionaires in 30 days or less. They go to seminars and training courses by the latest media gurus who promise instant happiness and enlightenment if they follow techniques practised by Oriental masters. It seems that some individuals have all the time in the world to search for short-cuts or a magic formula which will save them from making the required personal effort. Others aim to acquire manipulative techniques, psychological ploys and body-language skills to help them to succeed against other people. They rarely benefit from such knowledge if they regard these skills as tactics to be used on other people, instead of principles to be applied to their own growth.

In real life, principles are winners and tactics are losers when it comes to negotiating or working effectively with other people. There is no short-cut through the forest of life to the jewelled cavern – it takes patience, persistence and dogged determination. People may become personal growth butterflies who compete with each other to have read this or that book or to have attended the latest and trendiest seminars, like so many of the fad food diets that come and go.

Sadly, this is as far as it goes for many individuals, as they are putting their faith in a good fairy who will wave a magic wand over them or they are waiting for a spontaneous miracle to occur in their lives. All the available evidence fails to convince them that miracles are simply faith in action. Faith without determined thinking, speaking and action will achieve very little to bring about the changes that they wish to see happen in their lives.

The techniques and ideas that relate to individual personal growth will only work if we are determined to work at them long enough so that they become a part of our everyday routine. It is generally accepted that individuals who attend training courses paid for by their companies or other people derive far less benefit from them than a person who is committed to paying their own way.

I once attended a motivational seminar with some colleagues which was paid for by our employer and held at a prestigious city hotel. When the lift reached the sixth-floor conference room, one of my colleagues said that he had noticed that there was a bar on the tenth floor and that he was going there to get some real motivation instead of listening to a boring speaker. I doubt whether he would have done that if he had paid the fee for the one-day seminar out of his own pocket. I am doubly sure that he would not have done that if he had realized that the featured speaker was in the lift with us and that the seminar was being tape-recorded, with the participants receiving a personal copy of the proceedings. During the afternoon session, the speaker made a point of mentioning our colleague by name, saying how he assumed the red-haired lady he saw him leaving the hotel with must have been his wife. Needless to say, it cost our happily married colleague whose wife happened to be a brunette, much more than the seminar fee to buy up all our personal copies of the seminar tapes.

When recounting near-miraculous events in their lives, people often say how their prayers were answered and that they never gave up hope. They also say that they knew that if they kept on working, things would turn out all right in the end. Quiet achievers know that the real winners in life work at doing the tasks that others are able to do but are often unwilling to do.

The real losers in the game of life are those individuals who will not grasp the opportunity to work and study, or to learn new skills that will stand them in good stead for the future. People who are unable to do these things because of a difficult environment or because they are physically or mentally disadvantaged in some way, are by no means losers. They are the genuine heroes and heroines who have to struggle just to get to the starting line which many of us take for granted. Too many people give up prematurely on their own game of life by leaving the field to more determined players, while they retire to join all the other spectators, bystanders and critics on the sidelines. They still want to look, earn, travel and be like the active players in the game that they have voluntarily walked away from. They fantasize about being a winner at the game and to possess the same natural talent which made it so much easier for the people they would like to have been. It is highly unlikely, however, that they would accept a natural-born surgeon to operate on them or a natural-born lawyer to represent them in a court of law. They would insist first on tangible proof that these people had undergone years of rigorous training to achieve levels of competence recognized by their respective professional organizations. Through a strange process of mental gymnastics, they assume that film stars, television personalities, musicians, singers, comedians and their favourite sportspeople are naturally gifted and therefore exempt from sacrifice and effort. Most of these talented performers purposely cultivate an ordinary 'just like you' image because it appeals to the widest possible audience. This deceptive media image can mask the hard work and determination that it has taken to develop their talents to become anything but ordinary. Many of these successful individuals have achieved prominence by being single-minded, sacrificing many of the ordinary pleasures of everyday life that we take for granted. This passion to succeed against high odds in competitive fields can cause an imbalance in their lives which may lead them to suffer physical and psychological problems.

Whatever our personal view may be regarding the current level of social or economic activity in the Western world, there is absolutely nothing to stop us from accepting the principles outlined in this book and applying them to our lives. We each possess some self-esteem and have a measure of creative ability, and we should all accept a certain level of personal responsibility for our actions. We are relatively wise in some of our decisions and have a sense of purpose which we can communicate to others. We should have a measure of faith in our ability, therefore, to adapt to some changes in our lives and to be determined to achieve particular aims in life.

A young child may have exactly the same set of muscles as an adult weight-lifter. The difference lies not in the muscles but in the amount of concentrated development of those muscles which is needed to achieve a particular purpose. We are the only ones who can determine which principles are most in need of development for our unique life situation and we should strive to achieve a balance that is appropriate to our personality, aptitude and abilities.

It may be true that there is poverty, ignorance, bigotry and discrimination, together with apathy and injustice, in the world, but it is equally true that there is opportunity, an open access to information and lots of faith.

The quiet achievers recognize the fact that determination is the vital ingredient that helps them to achieve their goals. They understand and feel comfortable with an old saying which in essence goes something like this:

> Press on; nothing in the world can take the place of persistence. Talent will not; nothing is more common than unsuccessful individuals with talent. Genius will not; unrewarded genius is almost a proverb. Education will not; the world is full of educated derelicts. Persistence and determination alone are omnipotent.

10

—✦—

THIS WAY UP

Many people seem to possess the collector's mentality with regard to their own lives by trying to purchase a way of life or attempting to pursue or own happiness. These people fail to understand that you cannot buy life any more than you can earn, wear, consume or travel towards happiness. Life is not a continual striving after more and more material possessions or a constant searching for newer, more exotic physical sensations. It is about looking within ourselves to discover our real potential in life which lies waiting to be discovered and uncovered by each one of us. By changing the way we view ourselves and our possibilities in life, we begin to see the world around us in a new light. We then start to appreciate our true worth, our self-esteem improves and our imaginations begin to soar. This increased self-awareness leads us to appreciate our personal responsibility for continuing to learn as much as we can and for contributing as much as possible to life.

Real success is about relaxing at the end of a busy day and asking yourself whether you did marginally better today than yesterday in accomplishing the goals you have set for yourself. If you can honestly answer 'yes', give yourself a mental pat on the back. If the answer is an honest 'no', simply resolve to put more effort into your tasks tomorrow. Do not become downhearted if you slip back occasionally. It is the steady accumulation of small improvements that really counts, not giant leaps forward.

Success is not a frantic race against others where winning is all that counts. It is the general feeling of satisfaction that comes from knowing that we are simply doing our personal best. Successful living is not measured by how many trophies or awards we happen to collect and display along life's highway. We know that if anyone asks what we intend to leave behind us when we depart this world, we can answer truthfully, the same as Howard Hughes and John Paul Getty – 'Everything'!

Some individuals regard their life as a mere test because if it were the real thing, they would have been given all the answers to begin with. They are, in fact, half right. Life is a continual self-administered test to discover the answers to the questions that really count, and to keep our own scorecards about our progress throughout our lives. We should know and appreciate that this life is not simply a warm-up exercise for the main event which will happen in another time and place.

Life never seems to begin for some people as they have to clear a backlog of jobs, serve their time or repay their debts before they can really start to live. Eventually, some of them realize that these problems are their lives and that the situation can only improve if they decide to be better at living. We know that the common desire to outdo other people's achievements is really a sign of insecurity and immaturity which arises from allowing others to set the standards for our lives.

We will not know what our best will prove to be if we

choose to remain intelligently ignorant about the limits of our possible achievements. We should take a lesson from the bumblebee which, according to all the aero-dynamic expert evidence available, should not be able to fly. Although the bumblebee's body is far too heavy and its wings too small for flight, yet somehow it manages to fly regardless of its size.

Whatever we tell ourselves we want to do stems from the desire for the thing we have set our hearts and minds on and that desire motivates us to do something about it. Absolutely nothing happens without desire and, provided that what we want does not hurt others or ourselves, it is a signal of our capacity to achieve our objectives. A good test of the intention of our desire is to ask 'Is this what I would wish for everyone else I know?'.

The aim in living successfully is to build up in your mind and imagination a detailed mental image of the things you want and to erase images of the things you no longer desire. The quiet achievers know that nothing is frivolous in nature and they would not possess a desire for the good things of life if they were impossible to achieve. They do not regard it as a pleasant game of wishful thinking or simply of having a positive mental attitude. It is about right thinking. It involves using more of the right-side creative brain functions to become more balanced, whole brain thinkers.

We begin by focusing on what we really and truly want to achieve and listing these desires on paper. Once we are happy with this list, it is necessary to decide defi-nitely to accept the fulfilment of these desires as a reality here and now. It is not enough for the rational reasoning side of your mind to accept these messages; it requires the feeling side of your nature as well. We need to gener-ate the feelings of thankfulness and appreciation that we will experience upon obtaining our goal as if it were happening today. This is known as 'doing within' while you are 'doing without', and this potent combination of thinking and feeling has a powerful effect on the subconscious levels of the mind. Practised regularly, doing within while you are doing without and a belief in the fulfilment of your worthwhile desires, becomes a firm conviction.

These subjective convictions are strengthened by the use of the creative imagination, positive self-talk and relaxation on a daily basis. The subconscious mind is unable to think positively and negatively at the same time about any idea and any thoughts of lack, limitation and failure will gradually fade away.

We all tend to talk too much, even when we have conversations in our heads about our particular view of the world. We have only one mouth and two ears, so perhaps we should spend twice as much time listening to our true self as talking about what our two eyes can actually see. If we listen to our internal self-talk, we may discover that we are limiting our options by repeatedly telling ourselves the same unhelpful things about ourselves. We should also realize that when we stop talking internally about the world, it remains perfect, so perhaps we should start quietly listening to the world for a change.

The law of cause and effect is always in operation in our lives and is often known as the law of attraction and repulsion. This power or energy flows through us, picking up on our positive and negative thoughts, and helps to create the world we think about most often. This power is completely neutral and operates according to the current state of our thinking, arranging the outer world to conform to the inner workings of the mind. It is not interested in how many times we have made mistakes in the past, but if we continue to hold thoughts of bitterness, resentment and failure, it will oblige us like an innocent child by giving us more of the same in the future.

Most of us have managed to build up a store of negative images about ourselves and we may continue to feed them with negative thoughts, words and deeds. If this gang of juvenile mental delinquents has prevented us from loving what we do and doing what we love, it is going to take some determined use of our creative imaginations to evict them. In our mind's eye we should choose to see and feel ourselves enjoying our lives and moving steadily towards our desired goals for the benefit of ourselves and others.

The quiet achievers live their successful ideas on a daily basis by having a calmer, more confident attitude when operating in the mainstream of normal daily activities. They know that stress and strain reduces this flow of power like someone putting their foot on a garden hose and preventing the flow of water. They maintain, therefore, a relaxed attitude to all they do. They actively root out of their minds any negative feelings or grudges towards others, knowing that this will channel valuable energy away from their main aims in life. They realize that only they can work on their own consciousness because only they know what may be obstructing or diverting them from making more of their lives. If you believe that there is good and evil, they will manifest themselves for you; if you think that someone is preventing you from being successful, then probably they will. If you think that life is a roller-coaster – up one day and down the next, lots of money during the good times and precious little during the bad times – just remember that you become what you think about most.

If you are saying, 'it's all right for you to say that, but what about my lower back problems and my overdue mortgage payments and the awful people I have to work with everyday? You must be joking!', I can assure you in sincerity that I am not joking. It is totally possible that the condition of your financial affairs and your relationships with others can have a profound effect on your physical well-being. The personal experiences of quiet achievers have led them to believe completely in the power of the human mind to bring about desired changes in their lives. Only you can prove whether these methods will work for you or not by trying them for a reasonable length of time, maintaining an absolute faith in your convictions that it is possible.

If you fell into a river and were drowning, would you blame the water for your predicament or, more reasonably, the fact that you had not learned to swim properly? Whatever problems we are faced with, it is a waste of time and energy to blame the situation we may find ourselves in. We need to face up to the reality that, by accepting the common opinions of others as being facts about the way things really are, we are erecting hurdles which will slow down and impede our forward progress. The quiet achievers have removed those hurdles by making it a habit to visualize and affirm the good things which they want on a daily basis and by acting as if they already possessed them. Henry Wadsworth Longfellow wrote, 'Not in the clamour of the crowded street, not in the shouts and plaudits of the throng, but in ourselves are triumph and defeat.'

We know that we are what and where we are today because of what has entered our minds in the past. We know that, regardless of our past, tomorrow we have a clean slate to write on and what we write on it will determine our future. When we look back on our lives, what will we see? Will we have become the person we desired ourselves to be or will we be filled with regrets about missed opportunities to change the course of our lives for the better?

How we see life makes a vital difference to the corner of the world we inhabit, which leads us to cultivate the gardens of our minds through the constantly changing seasons of our life. We should accept that this work is a never-ending process of planting great ideas in our gardens and refusing others permission to plant them with insignificant thoughts. We should understand the impossibility of harvesting an abundant crop if we fail to water regularly and fertilize the seeds we have planted in our minds. We should tend our gardens with care, plucking out any stray weeds before they have a chance to take hold, thereby reducing the amount of nourishment that is available to the crop we intend to harvest in the due season.

The success and happiness which comes with a better life are not ends in themselves but a series of new beginnings every day of your life. Dare to be different by rising above poverty, sickness, strife and unfulfilled dreams by becoming the person you were really meant to be. Do not settle for a supporting role in other people's dramas – be yourself, be a star in your own right because this really is your life.

Make a quality decision to do something about it today and take the steps which other quiet achievers have taken before you, which will enable you to experience more of the wonder and joy of a better life. You have absolutely nothing to lose but everything to gain in the process, and you really do deserve the best that this life has to offer. Go ahead and try the various principles outlined in this book as they apply to your particular circumstances and influence the course of your life for the better.

Perhaps one day our paths may cross personally or you may write and tell me that you enjoyed reading this book, which would be a pleasurable experience for me. If you also added how it encouraged you to put some of these practical ideas to good use in your own life, that would be an equally satisfying experience for both of us.

FURTHER READING

Blue, L, & Magonet, J *Kindred Spirits*, Harper Collins, London, 1995

Drury, N, *The Elements of Human Potential*, Element Books, Shaftesbury, 1989

Goldsmith, J S, *The Infinite Way*, DeVorss & Co Publishers, California, 1947

Hariman, J, *How to Use the Power of Self-Hypnosis*, Thorsons, Wellingborough, 1981

Kaye, J L (ed), *Practical Wisdom for Perilous Times 'Selected Maxims of Baltasar Gracian'*, Harper Collins, London, 1994

Kornfiled, J, *Buddha's Little Instruction Book*, Bantam Doubleday Dell, New York, 1994

de Lubicz, I S, *The Opening of The Way*, Inner Traditions International Ltd., Vermont, 1981

Mandino, O, *A Better Way to Live*, Bantam Doubleday Dell, New York, 1990

Markham, U, *The Elements of Visualisation*, Element Books, Shaftesbury, 1989

Mulligan, J, *The Personal Management Handbook*, Macdonald & Co , London, 1988

Serebriakoff, V, *Test Your IQ*, Hamlyn, London, 1990

Strong, M, (ed), *Letters of The Scattered Brotherhood*, James Clarke & Co Ltd , Cambridge, 1965

Tart, C T, *Waking Up*, Element Books, Shaftesbury, 1988

Ziglar, Z, *Top Performance*, Fleming H Revell Company, New Jersey, 1986

INDEX